THE MATRIX MANUAL
FOR GUITAR

A Practical Approach to the Music You Want to Make

Craig D. Hillis, Ph.D.

CDH Productions
Austin, Texas
November 2021

INTRODUCTION

When I was a young pup wanting to play the guitar, I couldn't wait to strap on the new Kay six-string that my grandmother bought me, hop on the nearest stage, and let the good times roll. The last thing I wanted to do was sit in a small, stuffy room, look at a piece of paper with a bunch of intimidating little symbols plastered all over a series of parallel lines that was somehow supposed to translate into music on my new guitar. Reading music was something I always associated with piano lessons. I envisioned boring and repetitious exercises called scales and obediently listening to some sweet old gal with blue hair who had never even heard of Bob Dylan much less the Beatles or the Rolling Stones. That whole routine sounded way too much like studying and that's what school was for. I wanted to play right then and there. I wanted to create the cool sounds I was hearing on the radio. I wanted to rock!

This book is designed for those of you who identify with my early sentiments and want to get down to the business of playing. It's designed to provide you with the basic skills that will help you reproduce the songs and sounds that strike a special emotional chord in your life. It will provide you with the tools you need to create your own music and write your own songs. Ultimately, this book is about having fun on your own terms and if that leads to other grand musical adventures, well, that's great.

In addition to presenting the basic skills associated with the guitar, this book also tries to provide you with a working knowledge of the theoretical aspects of playing the instrument. Don't be alarmed. I'm not talking about "real" music theory with all the high-end subject matter associated with clefs, staves, notes, complex time signatures and the litany of intimidating words and phrases common to classical music studies. Rather, I'm talking about an accessible interpretation of music theory that I've developed over the years called the *Matrix Method*. Essentially, the *Matrix Method* draws on a series of generally accepted musical relationships based on a simple number system that resembles what many musicians call "Nashville Shorthand." I apply these common-sense relationships to the six strings and the fretboard of a standard guitar. This combination of strings and frets forms an elongated rectangle or matrix as seen here with the long vertical lines representing the strings and the short horizontal lines representing the frets.

THE BASIC MATRIX

This fundamental graphic format is the tool we'll use to illustrate how to play individual notes on the fretboard, how to combine those notes into harmonic clusters called chords, how to combine those chords into friendly groups called progressions, and how to use those progressions to play the songs you want to learn. Then, after we've got you rockin' on a few tunes, we'll use the same graphic format to highlight some of the "generally accepted musical relationships" I mentioned above and explore how all of this fits together into a tidy little package called "music" that I will explain in the *Matrix Method*.

We'll initially consider some basic information about the instrument, fingering techniques, fretboard and note mechanics, and tuning your guitar. These slightly tedious but necessary subjects will be covered in the following pages. There's quite a bit of information involved, so look it over, absorb what you can at your own pace and realize that you can refer back to various points as you move through the *Manual*. After the basic information section, we will get down to playing chords, making the sounds you want to hear, and creating the music you want to play. We will begin however with some basic explanations about this *Manual*, how it's designed and how it might work best for you.

The Matrix Manual for Guitar

The Matrix Manual for Guitar is divided into four chapters. The first
chapter briefly covers general information about the instrument, the structure of
chord charts, notes, tuning, and basic playing techniques. The second chapter
focuses on chords and chord progressions. The study of chord progressions
explains how individual notes come together in harmonic units to create chords,
how chords combine with other relevant chords to form progressions, and how
progressions provide the structural framework for popular songs. The third
chapter introduces the *Matrix Method* which is an interpretation of music theory
as it applies to the guitar. The *Matrix Method* highlights fundamental structural
relationships in music and explains them in accessible language. The fourth
chapter covers an extremely useful guitar technique, the barre chord system.
This technique opens the door to many new chords and alternative chord
positions that brings the entire fretboard into play.

As guitar manuals go, this is a long book. There are several reasons for
the *Manual's* length:

• I'm trying to be thorough in expressing the ideas, information, procedures,
and techniques associated with playing the guitar. I don't want to leave loose
ends or unresolved questions. Given that the medium at hand is the written word
rather than direct contact with the student, certain concepts require extended
discussions to properly relay the necessary information. What takes only a
minute to demonstrate and explain in a personal, one-on-one setting might take
several paragraphs to accurately convey on paper.

• The *Manual* is long because I include many topics beyond the scope of
most guitar-instruction books. Explaining the *Matrix Method* for example,
requires over twenty-five pages. Most guitar manuals for beginning students
don't address the broad scope of music theory much less a "plain-talk" version of
what can be intimidating musical concepts. The average "how-to" manual is
largely concerned with relaying the fundamental tools you'll need to play chords
and strum along to certain songs. They don't address the reasoning behind how
chords are formed, how they fit together with other chords to form progressions,

or how certain overriding concepts bring it all together in a unified approach to the instrument. This knowledge will prove extremely helpful in "speaking music" with your fellow players and band mates and will serve you well as you continue to advance in your studies and performance skills.

    • Other topics that contribute to the length of the *Manual* include aspects of music history as they relate to popular music trends, how sound works with technical information on sound waves, frequencies, and how such information relates directly to your guitar studies. Additionally, the *Manual* offers various overview charts on chord structures, scales and transposing from one key to another. Also featured throughout the text is a series of educational "Side Trips." These are essentially "mini-lessons" that expand on the information being covered or venture into to new, practical subjects that will enhance your ability to understand and play the guitar.

    • As a result of these and related features, the *Manual* is considerably longer, it's more detailed, and I would like to think, more accessible and helpful than other guitar instructional texts.

    As you work through the *Manual* you might notice that I repeat certain facts, lessons, and details time and again. I've certainly made this observation as I've read back through the document with an editor's eye, and from a literary point of view, I find such iteration somewhat bothersome. This Manual however is not a literary document; it's an instructional document. It is not designed to be read as one would read a novel or a collection of essays. As I suggested above, you will "*work* through the Manual;" you won't simply *read* through it. You might spend considerable time on a page or two as you apply the lessons presented in that section to the fretboard of your guitar. You might bounce from one section to another section, or you might revisit a certain section to clarify a point or to incorporate an aspect you've already covered into the lesson you're currently studying. I reasoned therefore that each section should, at least to some degree, be a "stand-alone" lesson and that requires repeating certain information from time to time. I apologize in advance if you find this redundant or tedious, but I though it better to err on the side of too much or repetitive information rather than leaving certain information out to satisfy literary conventions.

One last comment before we get started. From time to time, I'll be referring you to the Internet for examples of songs and other audio-visual representations of the subjects we're studying. This is in no way a requirement, but because I'm communicating with you through the written word, it's helpful to have the Internet as an audio-video support source. The Internet is an inexhaustible source of songs, complete with chord charts, tabs and performance videos. As I'll explain later, I'm unable to present comprehensive charts and lyrics for a great number of songs because of copyright and monetary considerations. Consequently, the Internet can be an extremely valuable support system by providing you with immediate examples of various subjects that appear throughout the *Manual*.

CHAPTER ONE
General Information

Anatomy of the Guitar

The Fretboard & The Chord Chart

Notes & Tuning

Playing Techniques

Anatomy of the Guitar

Here are the essential components of a standard steel-string guitar. There are a number of good, solid guitars available in today's market in the $150 to $250 price range. In getting started, it's important to have a guitar that's easy to play. "Easy to play" means an instrument that has a good "action." The "action" of a guitar refers to the distance between the strings and the fretboard. If the strings are too high, it makes the already challenging task of properly depressing the strings on the fretboard even harder. I strongly recommend that you take your instrument to a guitar tech and have it set up to insure maximum playability.

I would also suggest buying an electronic tuner. There are many different types, they are inexpensive and are very helpful in acquainting you with the way a particular string should sound when it's in tune. Even with with the tuner though, you will need to learn how to tune your guitar by ear, a technique we'll address in the following pages. This will come in handy when you've left your tuner at home. It will also help teach you how the notes are structured on the fret-board and the relationships between the various notes and strings.

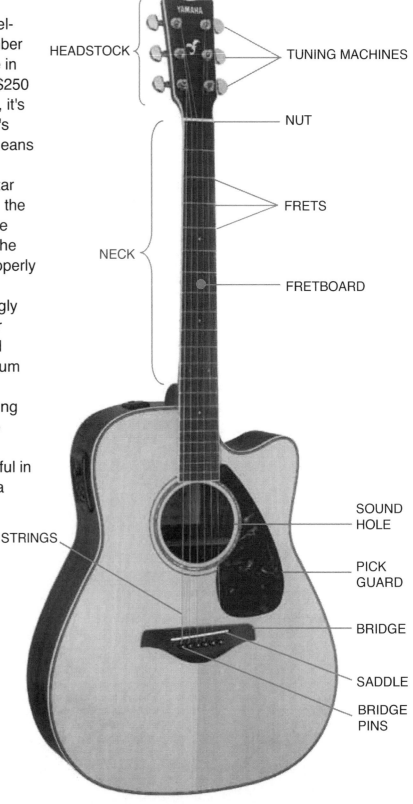

HEADSTOCK

TUNING MACHINES

NUT

FRETS

NECK

FRETBOARD

STRINGS

SOUND HOLE

PICK GUARD

BRIDGE

SADDLE

BRIDGE PINS

The Fretboard & The Chord Chart

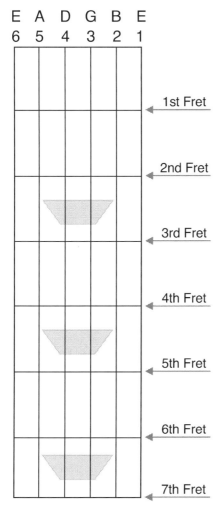

The graphic to the left represents the fretboard, the strings, and the frets. The small, inverted trapezoids represent fret markers commonly seen on the neck of most guitars. These fret markers come in all shapes, sizes and ornamental configurations.

The 6th string, the thickest string, is an E note, the 5th string is an A note, the 4th string is a D note, the 3rd string is a G note, the 2nd string is a B note, and the 1st string, the thinnest string and the string with the highest pitch, is another E note that rings with a significantly higher sound than the lower 6th string E note. The thickness of a string is known as its "gauge." The heavier gauge strings yield lower tones and the thinner gauge strings yield higher tones.

The frets are numbered accordingly. They begin with the first fret that is closest to the nut and move up the fretboard. Various types of guitars have different configurations of frets ranging from roughly 18 to 24 frets.

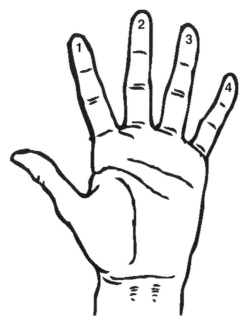

The illustration to the left simply shows how the four fingers are numbered from the Index to the Pinky. The chart to the right shows where the fingers are placed on the strings and the fretboard: The Index finger (1) is placed on the third string at the first fret; the Middle finger (2) on the fifth string at the second fret; and the Ring finger (3) on the fourth string at the second fret to form a basic "E" Chord.

Typical Chord Chart Illustrating an "E" Chord

9

Notes & Tuning

FILLING IN THE MATRIX

The chart to the right shows the various notes on the fretboard from the nut through the 12th fret. There are fundamental reasons why these notes unfold as they do, and we'll discuss those aspects later in the text. As you can see, the notes progress up the fretboard in alphabetical order with certain symbols between certain notes that represent sharps and flats. The symbol (#) represents a "sharp," so F# is an F-sharp note. The symbol (b) represents a "flat," so Gb is a G-flat note.

If you play the open 6th string, you're playing an E note. If you play the next note up at the 1st fret, you're playing an F note, and if you play the following note at the 2nd fret, you're playing an F-sharp (F#) or a G-flat (Gb). For reasons I'll explain later, the F# and the Gb (as well as many other flat and sharp notes) are the same tone yet are sometimes labeled differently.

If you play the open 5th string, you're playing an A note. If you play the next note up on the A string at the 1st fret, you're playing an A-sharp (A#) or a B-flat (Bb). If you play the following note at the 2nd fret, you're playing a B note. This type of sequencing holds true for all six strings up and down the fretboard.

Notice that after moving through twelve frets on any given open string, you arrive at the same note you began with except it rings at a considerably higher pitch. This is called an *octave*.

Note: Although I've not fully explained some of the technical relationships in this chart, these points will be covered in detail as we progress through the *Manual*.

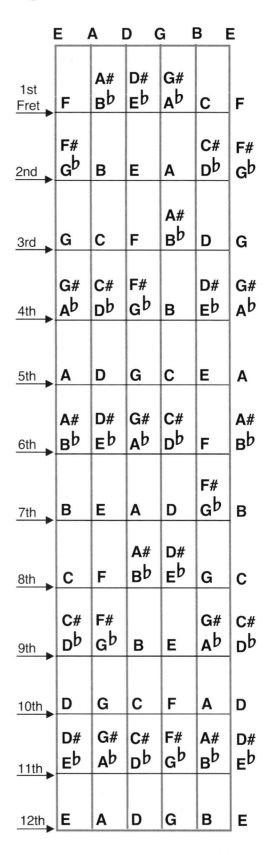

	E	A	D	G	B	E
1st Fret	F	A#/Bb	D#/Eb	G#/Ab	C	F
2nd	F#/Gb	B	E	A	C#/Db	F#/Gb
3rd	G	C	F	A#/Bb	D	G
4th	G#/Ab	C#/Db	F#/Gb	B	D#/Eb	G#/Ab
5th	A	D	G	C	E	A
6th	A#/Bb	D#/Eb	G#/Ab	C#/Db	F	A#/Bb
7th	B	E	A	D	F#/Gb	B
8th	C	F	A#/Bb	D#/Eb	G	C
9th	C#/Db	F#/Gb	B	E	G#/Ab	C#/Db
10th	D	G	C	F	A	D
11th	D#/Eb	G#/Ab	C#/Db	F#/Gb	A#/Bb	D#/Eb
12th	E	A	D	G	B	E

Notes & Tuning (*continued*)

There are two important concepts to be learned from the fretboard note display on the previous page.

The first concept has to do with the various notes which are the basic building blocks of music. The lowest note on the guitar is an E which is created by striking the open 6th string. And, as mentioned, if you move up twelve frets, you'll arrive at another E note (the octave) which is the higher-pitched version of the original E. But those aren't the only two E notes on the fretboard. There are numerous E as you move through the higher-pitched strings. The E note—as well as all the other notes—repeat and reappear because there are only twelve basic notes to work with! *That's worth saying again*: In the vast expanse of Western music whether you're playing a guitar, a trumpet, a piano, or a bassoon, *there are only twelve seminal notes*. All the great music from Beethoven to the Beatles and beyond is built on these same, essential building blocks . . . Twelve simple tones that I call the DNA of Western music.[1] Since we've been talking about the low E string, let's take the twelve notes on that string and lay them out in a line:

E	F	F# Gb	G	G# Ab	A	A# Bb	B	C	C# Db	D	D# Eb
1	2	3	4	5	6	7	8	9	10	11	12

Please note that "thirteenth" note—the note that would follow the D# - Eb—would be the E octave note.

The second concept demonstrates that these twelve seminal notes unfold in a continuous sequence much like the alphabet. In our E string example, the notes follow the alphabet except for those troublesome little sharp and flat notes that fall between most of the "regular alphabet" notes. In fact, the only time those "troublesome little sharps and flats" *don't* show up is between E and F and between B and C. That is simply the way musical notation has evolved through the centuries and has come down to us in the modern era. (More on this when we explore the *Matrix Method*.) The beauty of the system though, is that these odd rules are consistent from string to string up and down the fretboard. To illustrate, let's line out the notes on the A string just like we did with the E string:

---

[1] In speaking of "Western music," I'm referring largely to musics rooted in European or "Western" traditions dating back to the 11th century. This includes classical music and traditional ethnic musics that traveled to the New World beginning in the 16th century. "Western music" stands in contrast to the "Eastern" musics of Asia and the Middle East that often embrace different notes, scales, and rhythm signatures.

Notes & Tuning (*continued*)

	A# B♭	B	C	C# D♭	D	D# E♭	E	F	F# G♭	G	G# A♭
A											
1	2	3	4	5	6	7	8	9	10	11	12

(Again, the "thirteenth" note is the octave of the original note which would be an A note.)

The same note sequencing that's represented for the E and A strings above holds true for all the strings. A convenient way to wrap your mind around this concept of the consistent note sequence is to wrap the notes around a circle to form what might be called a "Note Clock." Since we just lined-out the notes on the A string, we'll position the A note at "high noon" and place the subsequent notes around the clock to complete the octave. In this fashion, you can begin at any starting point to run through a complete twelve-note sequence. If, for example, you were to begin at position "6" (which would be five o'clock on a standard clock face), you can trace the complete octave of the D string by traveling through the twelve positions.

The Note Clock

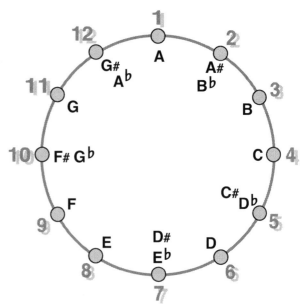

• Each position on the clock represents a single fret on the neck of the guitar and each fret represents a *half step*. A half step is the smallest interval in Western music scales. There are twelve half steps in one octave. Consequently, there's a half step between each of the notes in our DNA note sequence.

• Two half steps constitute a *whole step*. There is a whole step between all the "whole" tones. Whole tones are commonly considered those individual tones without a sharp or flat designation. In other words, there are whole steps between A & B; C & D; D & E; F & G; and G & A. **But...**

• There is always a half step between B & C and E & F. This is an important rule to keep in mind: Because there's a half step between B & C and E & F, we need not concern ourselves with a B# or a C♭ or an E# or an F♭.[2]

---

[2] Technically, in the more sophisticated world of music theory and notation, there can be a note *called* a B-sharp, a C-flat, an E-sharp, or an F-flat, but there is no true *tone* between the whole tones B & C and E & F. More on this in the *Matrix Method* Chapter.

Notes & Tuning (*continued*)

• Some closing thoughts on the Note Clock diagram: All the notes you'll ever need, all the notes that make up the DNA of Western music are displayed in that diagram. The *sequence* of notes is always the same. As mentioned, you can start at any position on the clock and map out a complete twelve-note "circular" octave in any key. Just like the clock, the same sequence unfolds on the strings of the guitar as you move from the lower pitched strings to the higher pitched strings. This brings us to the mechanics of tuning the guitar.

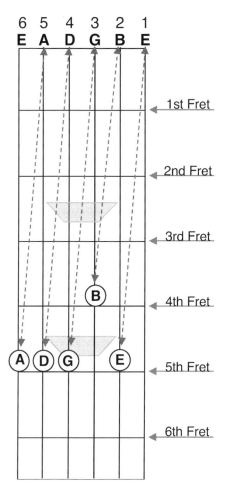

THE STANDARD GUITAR TUNING TECHNIQUE

• To begin the standard guitar tuning technique, start by tuning the 6th string to an E note. If you don't have someone to lend a hand with establishing the pitch of the E string, you can try to match it to an E note on the family piano or to a pitch pipe. If you have an electronic tuner, use it to tune the low E string. Now you can begin tuning the remaining five strings. Play an A note on the 6th string (I usually use my third finger but use whatever finger you're comfortable with). The A note is five frets (five half steps) up the neck. Play this A note then play the 5th string and tune it to duplicate the pitch of your "fifth-fret" A note. Use this same technique on the 5th (A) string to tune the 4th (D) string and repeat again on the 4th string to tune the 3rd (G) string. As you can see by the diagram to the left, the relationship between the 3rd (G) and the 2nd (B) string is different. You only need to go up four frets on the 3rd (G) string to produce the necessary B note to tune the 2nd string. Once the 2nd (B) string is in tune you can repeat the regular procedure by going up five frets on the 2nd (B) string to tune the 1st (E) string.

• You could use the electronic device to tune all the strings. But at this point, as a learning exercise, it's a good idea to use the standard tuning technique. Why? Because it will acquaint you with the way the various notes are supposed to sound. It will help you *train your ear*. My suggestion is to use the Standard Tuning Technique and check your work with the electronic device. This is the best of both worlds: It will ensure that you're playing in tune and that's the best "ear training" there is!

Playing Techniques

• **Fretting the Guitar**: When you depress a string to play a note, use the very tip of your finger. This will be a bit uncomfortable until you develop calluses on your left hand. In playing a note, position your finger as perpendicular as possible to the fretboard to avoid interfering with the neighboring strings. To produce a clear sounding note, place your finger directly behind the fret. Don't place your finger *on* the fret as it will mute the note, and don't place it too far *behind* the fret as the note will buzz.

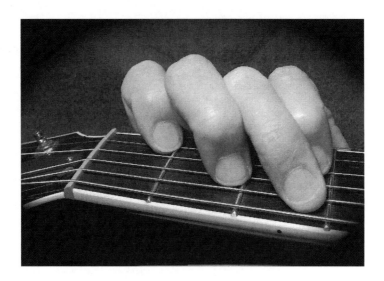

• **Using the Guitar Pick & Making Each Note Count**: There is nothing written in stone that says you must use a guitar pick, or, as it's often called, a "flatpick," but most guitar players do. There are certain guitar genres like classical or Flamingo that are performed exclusively with the thumb and fingers of the right (strumming) hand. There are other performance styles like "Cotton Picking" or "fingerpicking" that don't require a pick. But, as mentioned, most "pickers" use a pick! The image to the right is a standard guitar pick. Picks come in countless shapes and sizes, but the one to the right is the most common shape. Flatpicks also come in different thicknesses or "gauges." I recommend a medium or heavy pick in the standard shape to the right. On down the line, you might want to experiment with different types of picks. There are thumb picks and finger picks for example, or you might want to simply play with your fingers. At this point, as you're getting started, I'm hoping that you'll give the pick a try. Why? It will prove helpful in the process of learning chords and progressions by enabling you to single out and strike specific strings to make sure that all of the notes in your chord are sounding true and clean.

• The photographs below illustrate the standard technique of holding the pick. Make a relaxed fist with your right hand, place the pick on your index finger so the "point" of the pick projects out at a 90-degree angle from your thumb.

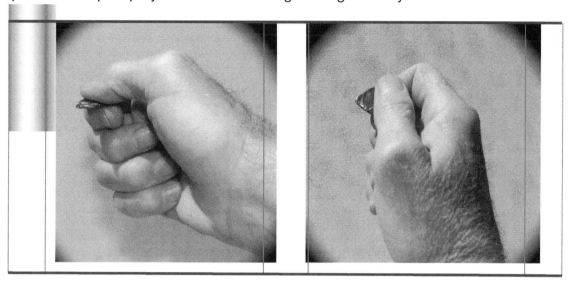

• It's not necessary to maintain an iron grip on the pick — Try to hold it loosely. This will enable you more flexibility in striking individual notes and playing multiple notes in a chord format. In playing individual notes, try to imagine that you're turning a key in a lock, twisting your fist from side to side. This will provide the abbreviated up and down strokes you'll eventually need in playing one note after another in a rapid sequence. In strumming chords, relax your right wrist and move your hand up and down and let your forearm follow that gentle back and forth movement. Ultimately, there's no right or wrong way to execute these various movements, just try to find a comfortable way that works for you.

CHAPTER TWO
Chords & Chord Progressions

Key of C
Basic Chord Progression
A "Minor" Side Trip - Major, Minor & Other Chord Designations

Key of D
Basic Chord Progression
A Side Trip - Transposing

Key of E
Basic Chord Progression
A Side Trip - Sevenths

Key of F
Basic Chord Progression
A Side Trip - Arpeggios

Key of G
Basic Chord Progression
A Side Trip - Pick & Strum

Key of A
Basic Chord Progression
A Side Trip - Suspended Chords

Key of B
Basic Chord Progression
A Side Trip - Time & Tempo

Chords & Chord Progressions

Behind almost any popular song is a chord progression. Regardless of the genre or the style—rock, country, folk, gospel, rockabilly, western swing, hip-hop, reggae, blues, bluegrass, be-bop or jazz—popular songs are largely based on chord progressions. I'm differentiating between "popular" songs and classical music which is infinitely more complicated. Still, there are countless examples of chord progressions laced throughout the work of the classical masters. Chord progressions lie at the heart of the 19th-century Stephen Foster American classics, the John Phillip Sousa patriotic marches, the early 20th-century Ragtime compositions of Scott Joplin, the 1920s Dixieland improvisations, the 1930s Broadway hits, the 1940s big-band dance tunes, the 1950s & 60s Sinatra ballads, and the Beach-Blanket-Bingo surfing instrumentals! The majority of the popular songs that defines our contemporary tastes and cultural sensibilities are built on the sturdy bones of the chord progression.

So, just what are these all-powerful "chord progressions?" We'll address the technical and theoretical side of chords and progressions later in the *Manual*, but for the time being, here are some nontechnical definitions that will be helpful:

 • A **chord** is a small cluster of notes built around three primary tones that sound compatible and pleasing to the ear. Chords are essentially little families of harmonious notes.

 • A **progression** is based on three compatible chords that sound natural when played in sequence. Just as chords are little families of harmonious single notes, progression are families of complimentary chords.

 • Every individual note on the circular illustration or Note Clock on page 12 represents a specific "key," and every key has its own family of harmonious chords which characterize that specific progression. Accordingly, there is an A progression, an A# or B♭ progression, a B progression, a C progression, a C# or D♭ progression and so on.

 • There are various structural reasons why chords and progressions fit together the way they do but we'll save that technical analysis for the forthcoming *Matrix Method* chapter. At this point, it's important to recognize that there are certain groups of chords that work well together, chords that occupy the same harmonic space that are responsible for making our favorite songs sound familiar and accessible.

In the pages that follow, I'll chart out a series of progressions based on the whole tones featured on the Note Clock on page 12. By "whole tones" I'm referring to the notes that are *not* sharp or flat notes. The whole tones and their subsequent progressions are A, B, C, D, E, F, and G. A treatment of progressions based on flat and sharp keys appears later in the Manual on page 142.

• **Presenting the Progressions with a Few Side Trips**: Many of the "How to Play the Guitar" books I've reviewed simply lay out the chords associated with a particular progression. Other publications dig a little deeper and use traditional musical terminology to label the three primary chords in a progression. Using the C Progression as an example, let's explore some of the aspects of this this labeling process:

    • To assist in understanding this labeling process, I've charted the 7 notes of the **C Scale** below. Notice that there are 8 notes if you count the last note of the scale which is another C note that's an octave higher than the original C. Please note that a *scale* is significantly different from the list of sequential notes on the Note Clock or the "note lines" referenced above. This is because the structure of a seven-note scale requires specific "intervals" or "steps" between the notes. In other words, to create a scale, specific notes are referenced from the note clock or on the note line. Some of the intervals between the notes of the scale are whole steps while other intervals are half steps. I'll explain the creation of scales in the *Matrix Method* section, but for now, let's define the notes of the C scale:

Notes of the C Scale:	C	D	E	F	G	A	B	C
Position in the Scale:	1	2	3	4	5	6	7	8

    • The first chord in any particular progression, the chord that shares the name of that progression is the "**Tonic**" chord. The Tonic is the chord built around the **1st note** of the scale, the C note in this case. This chord is also called the "**I**" (one) chord because it falls on the first position of the scale.
    • The second primary chord in the progression is the "**Subdominant**" chord and is built around the **4th note** (F) of the scale. This chord is also called the "**IV**" (four) chord because it falls on the fourth position of the scale.
    • The third primary chord in the progression is the "**Dominant**" chord and is built around the **5th note** (G) of the scale. This chord is also called the "**V**" (five) chord because it falls on the fifth position of the scale.
    • This is all valuable information and as I mentioned, we'll take a closer look at these structural relationships later in the text. At this point though, I'd like to comment on what I'm calling **Side Trips**.
    Included in the sections on chord progressions will be informative segments that will be helpful in the learning process. I mention this in advance because these so-called Side Trips feature subjects that aren't commonly presented in the context of exploring chord progressions in most guitar

instruction books. The subjects of these side trips relate to all the progressions, not just the progression in which they appear. As you'll see, they are helpful tools of the trade and will significantly expand your ability to recreate the popular songs and sounds you like and put you on the path to writing your own material.

• In presenting the C Progression for example, I'll introduce the concept of the minor chord and explain that every progression has a "relative minor" chord.

• With the D Progression we'll touch on the mechanics of *transposing*. Transposing in a music setting essentially means moving a song or a sequence from one key to another. Say for example, you're playing a song in the key of E and it's too low for the vocalist. You can transpose the song to a higher key like F or G to accommodate the performer's vocal range.

• With the E Progression we'll take a look at seventh chords. Seventh chords, like minors and other chord types, have a unique sound and play a distinct role in making music.

• In discussing the F Progression we'll consider arpeggios. To play an arpeggio is to play the notes of a chord in succession either in an ascending or descending fashion. In practical terms it means to pick out the individual notes of a chord rather than strumming the chord.

• With the G Progression we'll try a new strumming technique called "Pick & Strum." This is a combination of playing individual notes while strumming chords.

• With the A Progression we'll have some fun with "suspended" chords. These are chords that play a notable role in many popular hit songs and that add a unique flavor to many progressions.

• In the B Progression we'll explore the basics of timing and tempo. Keeping proper time is extremely important to reproduce songs and musical passages as they were written and to play effectively in ensemble settings with other musicians.

Key of C · Basic Chord Progression

The first progression we'll consider is the C Progression. This is a very common progression that's relatively easy to play. The three basic chords in the C Progression are the **C** chord, the **F** chord, and the **G** chord. There are other chords relevant to this progression, but we'll address those later as we move through the *Manual*. We'll get started by explaining the proper way to play a C chord.   pply the sam   s to the **F** ch

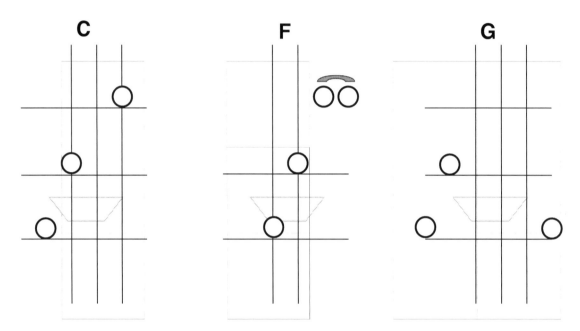

• **The C Chord**: Start by positioning the first finger of your left hand on the 2nd string at the 1st fret.[3] Next, place your second finger on the 3rd string at the 2nd fret. Then, stretch out your third finger and place it on the 5th string at the 3rd fret. Make sure that you place your fingers directly behind the appropriate frets and try to push down on the strings with the tips of your fingers. I realize that this might be a little uncomfortable, but it's important to apply steady pressure on the strings. It might help if you place the thumb of your "fretting" hand on the back of the neck so you can pinch the neck and apply more pressure to your "fretting" fingers. Also, notice that there's an **X** above the 6th string. This means that you don't play that string.

---

[3] If you're left-handed, try incorporating the techniques used by right-handed players. Most beginning guitar students who are right-handed have *two left hands*, and those who are left-handed have *two right hands*! If fretting the instrument is uncomfortable with your left hand, don't worry. Simply finger the chords with your right hand and realize that the higher-pitched strings are on the top of the string sequence and that you might have to modify your strumming techniques.

• You are now ready to strum the **C** chord. Position the flatpick comfortably in your strumming hand and beginning with the 5th string, play each individual string to make sure the notes you're holding down sound clear and true. Also, make sure that the open strings sound clear and true. It's very easy to relax one of your fretting fingers and mute a string.

• After playing the individual strings, strum all five strings and get a feel for the way it feels and sounds. Again, make sure that each note is ringing through crisp and clear.

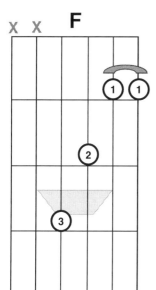

• **The F Chord**: This chord requires a little extra effort because you'll have to play two strings with one finger. Begin by placing your first finger flat on the fretboard to depress the 1st and 2nd strings at the 1st fret. The arch over the 1st and 2nd strings in the illustration represents one finger playing multiple strings. Place your second finger on the 3rd string at the 2nd fret. Finish the chord by placing your third finger on the 4th string at the 3rd fret. Please notice the **X** over the 5th string and the **X** over the 6th string. Don't play these strings.

• Starting with the 4th string, play each individual string to make sure your notes ring clear and true. This is a challenging configuration, so be patient and try to apply enough pressure on the strings. Also, make sure your fingers are placed immediately behind the frets.

• Again, try strumming all four strings. I realize that this is a bit of a challenge because you're not playing the 5th and the 6th string. Exercise by strumming down then back up and you'll soon get a feel for playing just the four notes of the chord.

• **The G Chord**: Begin by placing your first finger on the 5th string at the 2nd fret, place your second finger on the 6th string at the 3rd fret, and finish the chord by placing your third finger on the 1st string at the 3rd fret. Notice that with the **G** chord, you're playing all 6 strings. Pick the individual strings to ensure clarity and try a few full strums.

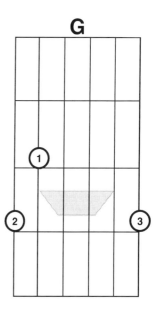

• **Playing Your Progression**: Now try playing the three chords in sequence. Begin with the **C** chord, strum it a few times, then move to the **F** for a few strums, then on to the **G** for a few more. Mix the chords up and try playing them in different sequences. When you begin to get the hang of forming the chords, try playing each one a specific number of times, four times on each for example, and move from the **C** to the **F** to the **G** then back to the **F** and finally back to the **C**. Continue this pattern for a few passes. You are now putting your progression to work, and believe it or not, you have just learned how to play thousands of songs!

• As an example of one of these "thousands of songs," let's try a simple hymn, "Amazing Grace," by the 18th-century English poet and clergyman, John Newton, published in 1779. It's a well-known song that illustrates how three simple chords can come together to create a tune that has endured for over 200 years. The chords are situated above the lyrics and the diagonal lines underneath the lyrics represent a single strum of the chord. Try to strum each chord in a steady rhythm . . . (C) 1, 2, 3, 4 - (F) 1, 2, 3, 4 - (G) 1, 2, 3, 4 etc. Also, I've tried to align the words and syllables with the sequence of the strums or beats represented by the diagonal lines. In the beginning of the song for example, notice that the first strum starts on the second syllable of the first word (A - _maz_ - ing). Also, as the tune develops, the lyrics are spread out to correspond with the strums and beats.

> "Amazing Grace" is one of many three-chord songs that's easy to learn. For similar songs, search the Internet for _three-chord songs_. Select some of these that you like and try playing them. As we explore other progressions, you'll find that you can play these new songs in different keys.

```
  C                    F        C
A - mazing   Grace, how sweet the   sound,
  / / / / / / / /  / / / /  / / / /
  C                   G
That saved   a   wretch  like me.
    / / / /   / / / /  / / / / / / / /
  C                    F        C
I once    was lost,    but now    I'm  found,
 / / / /  / / / /  / / / / / / /
  C        G          C
Was blind   but now     I  see
   / / / / / / / / / / / /
```

• **Introducing the minor chord**: Let me introduce another chord that's an important element of the C Progression. This new chord is the A-minor chord (**Am**) and will enable you to play even more songs. To play the **Am** chord, begin by placing your first finger on the 2nd string at the 1st fret, then place your second finger on the 4th string at the 2nd fret, and finally, place your third finger on the 3rd string at the 2nd fret. Having learned the Am chord, we'll now consider the significance of minor chords that applies to all of the chord progressions.

Am

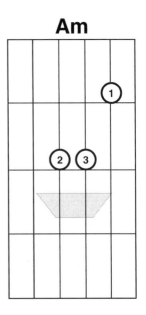

• **A "Minor" Side Trip - Major, Minor and Other Chord Designations**: The three primary chords of the C Progression—**C**, **F** and **G**—are all major chords. There are structural reasons why these note combinations are known as "major" chords, just as there are reasons why there are "minor" chords. Once again, we'll save these technicalities for the *Matrix Method* chapter, but for now, I'll present a few "audio observations" about these chords.

• By "audio observations" I'm referring to how chords sound and how those sounds work together in a progression. If, for example, I was to tell you that the difference between a major chord and a minor chord is a "flatted third," that probably wouldn't be very helpful. Consequently, I'm going to try to relay how various chords *feel* and how they evoke emotions in both the player and the listener. The following descriptions are subjective, but they are based on a long history of how chords are used to create moods and emotions.

• **Major chords** sound happy and often portray up-beat emotions. A good example of this is "Happy Birthday," which, by the way, you can now play with the three basic chords of the C Progression:

```
         C                        G
Happy Birth - day   to      you        Happy
        /        /       /        /         /        /
G                        C
Birth - day    to        you             Happy
/        /        /        /        /        /        /
C                        F
Birth - day    dear    Humanoid          Happy
/        /        /        /        /        /        /
C              G        C
Birth - day    to       you.
/        /        /        /        /        /        /
```

> Major chords don't automatically suggest a specific emotional response. Songs centered on major chords run the gamut of emotions and subject matter. It might be more accurate to say that major chords have a neutral quality particularly when contrasted to minor chords that have an identifiable darker texture.

• **Minor Chords** portray a different feel. They suggest a more somber, even dark feel. Many folks refer to the minor chords as "blue" chords because they're often associated with blues songs and frankly, they often sound emotionally "blue" in the proper context. Try playing the **C** chord followed by the **Am** chord and you'll be able to sense the different feel and texture of the **Am** chord. Musical scores for motion pictures provide a good example of how major chords and minor chords suggest different emotions. If there's up-beat action on the screen or if the characters are engaged in positive behavior, chances are the composer is relying on major-chord themes for the score. If the action takes a sinister turn, if the "bad guy" appears, or if there's a sad or suspenseful scene, chances are the composer is relying on minor-chord themes for the score.

• **The Relative Minor Chord**: Every progression has a "relative minor" chord. The *relative* minor chord is the minor chord that is most commonly associated with a particular progression. **Am** is the relative minor for the C Progression. There are other minor chords associated with the C Progression (or, for that matter, with any progression), but the relative minor chord is the "go-to" minor chord in any particular progression. Let's now integrate the **Am** chord into the C Progression, put it in the context of some popular songs, and see how this *relative minor* business works. First, I'll chart the four chords you'll be working with and lay them out in the order that you'll be playing them:

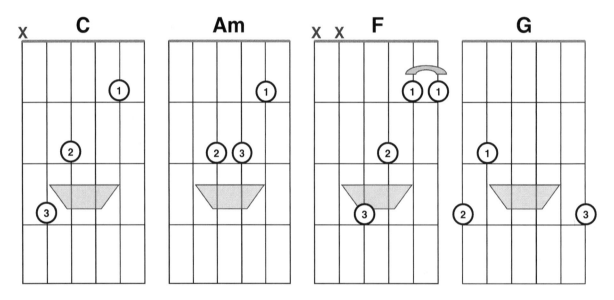

Now try playing these four chords in sequence strumming each chord four times. Start very slowly and try to make sure that all of the notes of the individual chords are crisp and clear. Keep in mind that with the **C** chord and the **F** chord that there are certain lower notes that you don't play. A very important consideration at this point is to strive for a steady rhythm as you move through these chords. Moving from one chord to the next in a timely, steady fashion is tough, and it's going to take patience and practice. Charting this exercise would look like this:

After completing this four chord-sixteen beat sequence, repeat it again and again until it begins to settle into a smooth groove. Now try to move through the chord sequence more quickly by strumming each chord only twice:

```
C       Am      F       G       C       Am      F       G
/   /   /   /   /   /   /   /   /   /   /   /   /   /   /   /
```

Again, keep running over the sequence and try to tighten up the chord changes on every new pass. This is challenging work, but soon you'll be able to pass from one chord to another while maintaining a steady beat. When you get your rhythmic groove down, you might notice that this **C-Am-F-G** chord progression sounds familiar. It should! This basic chord structure provides the nuts 'n' bolts for countless popular hits! I will offer a few examples shortly.

• **Some Thoughts on the C-Am-F-G Sequence**: This chord sequence is simply a subset of the C Progression. It's a product of the three primary chords—**C**, **F**, and **G** with the addition of the relative minor. In the key of C, the relative minor is **Am**. Every chord progression, whether it's an A, A#-B*b*, B, C, C#-D*b*, D etc., has its own relative minor. Also, every chord progression has its own version of the **C-Am-F-G** sequence. As we will see when we address the Key of G, the sequence that mirrors the **C-Am-F-G** structure features these chords: **G-Em-C-D**. Accordingly, any songs that you learn using **C-Am-F-G**, you can easily *transpose* to the key of G by substituting the "mirror chords" of **G-Em-C-D**. To "transpose" a set of chords is to play that same chord sequence in a different key. This applies to all progressions in all keys. You'll find the transposing process helpful in singing songs. If a particular key is too high or too low to sing along with, you can transpose the song to a more comfortable key. For more information on transposing, see page 28.

• **Some "Historical" Thoughts on the C-Am-F-G Progression**: This chord sequence in C and, by extension, its counterpart in all the other keys, has been around for hundreds of years. Musical compositions from the Renaissance to the present have used this particular sequence in countless songs and musical arrangements. The **C-Am-F-G** structure and its structural cousins in other keys became extremely popular in the 1950s and 1960s when popular songwriters began cranking out "doo-wop" songs and top-ten radio hits sung by vocal groups like The Penguins ("Earth Angel"), The Drifters ("This Magic Moment"), The Marvelettes ("Please Mr. Postman"), and the Everly Brothers ("All I Have to Do Is Dream"). Many single artists like Sam Cooke ("Chain Gang"), Gene Chandler ("Duke of Earl"), and Ben E. King ("Stand by Me") had huge hits with this progression. Retrospectively, the sequence has come to be known as the "1950s Progression," the "Oldies Progression," and sometimes, the "Ice Cream Changes," which was probably a reference to the malt shops that were so popular during the 1950s. The trend continued as many early 1960s folk groups covered songs written by Pete Seeger like "Where Have All the Flowers Gone," and "If I Had a Hammer," and even super groups like the Beatles incorporated the progression into tunes like "Happiness Is a Warm Gun", and "Octopus's Garden."

I suggest that you visit the Internet and search for "**C-Am-F-G Songs**." You'll find many titles you'll recognize. Many of these selections are accompanied by chord charts and/or instructional videos. Once you can play **C-Am-F-G** in a steady rhythmic sequence, try rearranging the sequence of the chords in this fashion: Start with the C chord, then go to the G chord, followed by the Am chord and finish with the F chord. This particular sequence — **C-G-Am-F** — is often called the "Pop-Punk Chord Progression," and yields an entirely new selection of tunes and popular artists. Some highly popular examples include "Beast of Burden" by the Rolling Stones, "Don't Stop Believing" by Journey, and "Let It Be" by the Beatles. Again, search the Internet for "**C-G-Am-F Songs**" and see what you can find!

There are two reasons why I'm not giving you examples of these songs in the text: First, I don't know what kind of music you like. There are so many examples of this basic C-Am-F-G sequence (and the C-G-Am-F sequence), I'm afraid I'd choose a song that you've never heard! It might be better for you to choose one from the Internet that you like and try to apply the progression to a familiar tune.

Second, there are copyright considerations that apply to the use of popular songs in instruction manuals like this one. If I were to feature a hit song, chart the chords, and print the lyrics, I would have to pay the songwriter and publisher a statutory fee. As a songwriter myself, I'm all in favor of that! But to use a collection of mega-hits that most folks would recognize can be very expensive for a simple publication like this one.

For these reasons, the examples I use in this text are in the "Public Domain." Public Domain refers to songs that anyone can freely use without having to pay the fees associated with songs that are privately owned and published by commercial enterprises. Public Domain songs are often older songs or traditional songs where there is no clear record of authorship. Public Domain songs also include titles that have moved beyond their statutory timeline of copyright coverage. Older copyright laws established definite "periods of coverage," and when that time ran out, certain songs moved into the Public Domain. "Amazing Grace" and "Happy Birthday" are examples of Public Domain songs.

Public Domain songs are often pieces that most people have heard. They may not be enshrined in the Rock 'n' Roll or the Country Music Hall of Fame, but they are generally known to many generations of Americans.

Key of D · Basic Chord Progression

The next progression is the D Progression. We began with the C Progression, so we'll continue through the Progressions & Keys in alphabetic order. The three basic chords in the D Progression are **D**, **G**, and **A**. We will also introduce the **Bm** chord which is the relative minor for the D Progression. First, here are the illustrations for the three primary chords in the Key of **D**:

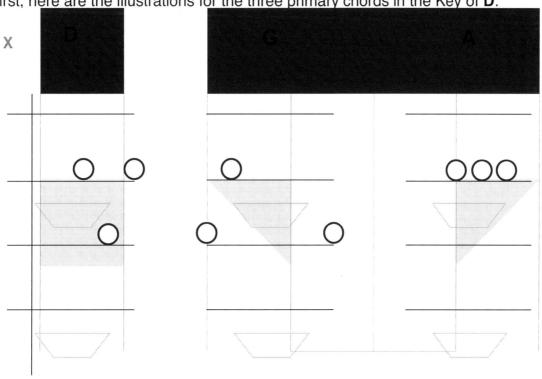

• The finger positions for the **D** chord are relatively simple. I've always pictured this chord as a small triangle! Sometimes it's helpful to envision chords as geometric shapes to help remember them. Please note that you don't play the 6th string.

• We addressed the second chord, **G**, in learning the C Progression. The repeat of the **G** chord brings up an important point: Certain chords will resurface as we work through new progressions in different keys. Remember, we're drawing from a limited inventory of notes. There are only twelve seminal notes in the grand designed that I'm calling the "DNA of Western Music." Because there are twelve notes, there are twelve progressions in twelve different keys. You might find it helpful to refer to the "Note Clock" on page 12 that depicts all the notes. This finite number of building blocks that continue in a perpetual circle suggests that many of the same chords will resurface as we move through new chord progressions.

• The third primary chord of the D Progression, **A**, requires a bit of "finger dexterity." You must squeeze together your first, second, and third fingers on the 4th, 3rd, and 2nd strings at the second fret as illustrated in the chord chart above. Most challenging chords require stretching your fingers to make the formation, but in this case, you must crunch them together. Some guitar players use a single finger to play this chord, but we'll address that technique later in the text.

• The relative minor for the D progression is **Bm**. Forming the **Bm** chord is new territory because we're moving several frets up the neck to play the chord. Begin building the chord by placing your first finger on the 1st string at the 2nd fret then follow the fingering positions presented in the illustration to the right.

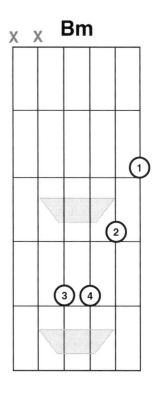

Please note that you don't play the low E (6th) string or the A (5th) string. Playing only four strings is always a bit difficult. We all have a tendency to blast away on all six strings but try to focus only on the last four strings so the chord rings clear and true. Later on, we'll address a new method of expanding certain "four-string" chords like **Bm** and **F** to involve all six strings. This technique is based on the concept of the "barre chord." A "barre chord" involves using your first finger to form a "barre" across all six strings so you can incorporate all the strings into the chord. For now, please be patient and focus on playing a crisp four-string **Bm** chord.

• **Putting the D Progression to Work**: To get a feel for this progression, try the exercise you used with the C Progression (C, Am, F, G): Move through the D Progression chords in this order, **D**, **Bm**, **G**, **A**, and strum each chord four times. You're obviously substituting your D Progression chords for your C Progression chords. In other words, you're *transposing* a chord structure from the key of **C** to the key of **D**.

D	Bm	G	A

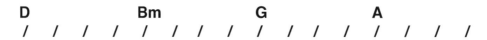

Going from the **D** to the **Bm** is difficult but dig in and give it a go. The changes from **G** to **A** and back to **D** are a little easier to make. Once you feel comfortable with these chords, try to run through the sequence at a measured pace. If that means moving very slowly, that's fine! The main objective is to concentrate on making the changes at a steady, deliberate pace. Your tempo will pick up with practice. Once this exercising is moving smoothly, try doubling up on the chord sequence like you did in the C Progression exercise. Strum each chord for two beats rather four beats:

D		Bm		G		A		D		Bm		G		A	
/	/	/	/	/	/	/	/	/	/	/	/	/	/	/	/

As you tighten up your chord changes and lay them down in a stead groove, you'll notice that the harmonic structure—which is to say, how the chords sound together in a particular structure—is very much like the **C-Am-F-G** sequence you were playing earlier. I hinted at this above in speaking about transposing from one key to another. Let's take a minute to check out how this transposition business actually works.

• **A Side Trip - Transposing**: From a technical perspective, transposing is the process of moving the pitch of a collection of notes, musical phrases, or complete songs to another key while maintaining constant tone intervals. In practical terms, it's the process of moving a piece of music from one key to another and keeping the structure intact. The mechanics of the transposition process is rooted in the way the notes are laid out on the fretboard of the guitar. The inventory of notes is displayed in a circular fashion on the note clock and in a linear fashion on the "fretboard matrix." Before offering examples of transposing, I'm reintroducing the Note Clock as a convenient reference:

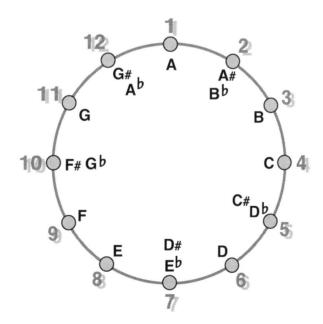

29

By using this illustration, we can choose a specific note as a starting point and follow all the subsequent notes around the circle until we arrive back at our original note. Because we started with the C Progression, we're going to take all of the notes that follow the C note beginning at "three o'clock" and lay them out in a line. Then we'll take all the notes that follow the D note beginning at "five o'clock" and lay them out in a line. In this fashion is easy to compare the sequence of C notes (and chords) with the sequence of D notes (and chords):

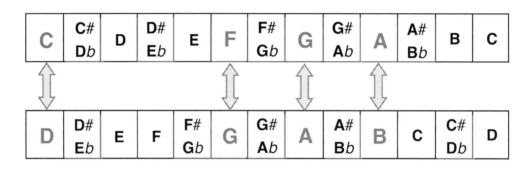

This comparison illustrates how the two lines of sequential notes in two different keys relate to each other and the ease with which a player can move from one key to another. This graphic serves as a Transposition Chart that readily shows the player how to take the C - Am - F - G sequence and it to the Key of D by substituting D - Bm - G - A.

Later in the *Manual* I'll present a master Transposition Chart that features all the different keys.[4] Before getting to that though, we'll need to analyze the relationship between a sequence of **notes** and a **scale**. This is an important consideration. A list of notes as they appear on the guitar neck (as illustrated above) is not the same thing as a **scale**. A scale is built from this sequence of notes but there is a special system of intervals—whole steps and half steps—that constitute a scale. We'll address the mechanics of scales later! Right now, let's move on to another progression and some new chords.

---

[4] The Transposition Chart appears in the Summary Section of the Matrix Method on page 103.

Key of E · Basic Chord Progression

For all of you rock 'n' roll fans, this is an important progression. There are scores of rock songs in the key of E. As a young 1960s rocker, I found that many of the "classics" were in the Key of E—"Gloria," "For What It's Worth," "Born on the Bayou," "Satisfaction," and others. Even in the second decade of the 21st century, the E Progression is still going strong! Here are the three primary chords   ar progressi

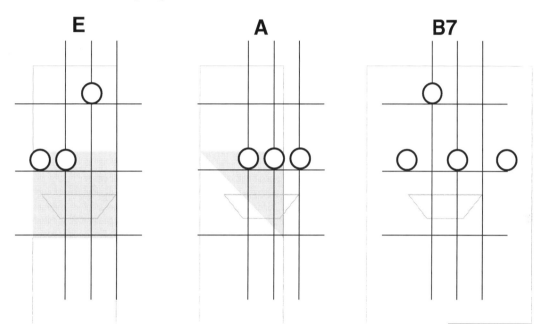

We mentioned the E chord earlier, we've covere the A chord, and the B7 (B-Seventh) chord is not very difficult. Form a small triangle with your first, second, a third fingers as depicted in the chart, then place your fourth finger on the 1st string at the 2nd fret. Also, plea note that you don't play the 6th string. Unlike previous progressions, one of the primary chords is a 7th Chord. This is the first 7th chord we've encountered. This B7 could just as easily have been a regular B chord, but m instructional texts use the B7 as the V (five) or "Domina chord for the E Progression. Why? Probably because B7 is easier to play than a standard B chord (see right). To play the B, situate your first finger on the 1st string a the 2nd fret, then make what amounts to an A chord formation on the 4th fret. What you've essentially done to move the A chord up two frets (or two half steps) to

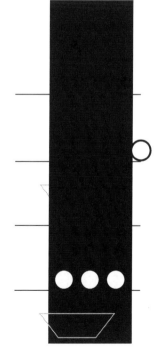

The relative minor for the E Progression, Dbm (D-flat minor) is a tough chord to play. Unfortunately, there aren't any "finger friendly" versions of the Dbm without using a barre chord. To form this minor chord, place your first finger on the 1st string at the fourth fret, then place your second finger on the 2nd string at the fifth fret. Reach over with your third finger and place it on the 4th string at the sixth fret, then snuggle your fourth finger next-door on the 3rd string also at the sixth fret. Be careful not to play the 5th and 6th strings.

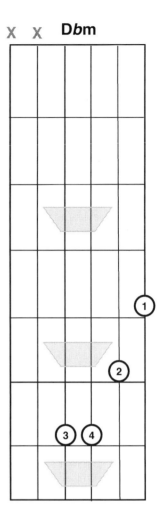

Interestingly, many of the classic pop songs rooted in the E Progression don't depend too heavily on the relative minor. The songs I mentioned above for example, don't include the Dbm chord. Still, I strongly recommend that you include this relative minor chord in your E Progression practice sessions. Mastering this chord as well as other "tedious" chord constructions will serve you well when we tackle the barre chord techniques in Chapter Four.

For fun, for old time's sake, *and* to give you some new insights into song structures, I'm going to introduce another chord that is often associated with the E Progression. It is a chord we have already studied, "D."

As I mentioned, the "E-based" songs, "Gloria," "For What It's Worth," "Satisfaction," and "Born on the Bayou" don't include the relative minor, Dbm. They do however prominently feature the D chord. A good way to understand the role of the D chord in this context is to study a handy group of chords that surfaces again and again in popular rock songs. Those chords are, **E**, **D** and **A**. To get a feel for how these chords sound together, we will try two brief exercises.

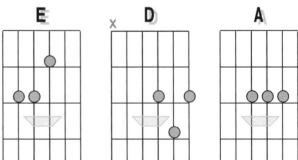

• First, strum the E chord four times, strum the D chord two times, strum the A chord two times, then move back to the E chord and begin the process again. The chart below illustrates two cycles of this chord combination. Play through the chords until you can maintain a slow but steady pace.

E   D   A   E   D   A

/   /   /   /   /   /   /   /   /   /   /   /   /   /   /   /

Once you feel comfortable with the initial exercise, try to tighten up the chord changes by strumming the E chord only two times, the D chord one time, and the A chord one time. Repeat the sequence until you establish a steady groove.

E   D   A   E   D   A   E   D   A   E   D   A

/   /   /   /   /   /   /   /   /   /   /   /   /   /   /   /

As you move toward your "steady groove," I'm hoping these chords might start to sound familiar. This particular chord sequence is the basic rhythm guitar pattern for the pop song, "Gloria." As you experiment with different configurations of the E, the D, and the A chord, there will be other songs that come to mind. You might try an Internet search with the key words, "Songs with E, D, A." I'm betting that you'll discover several songs on your personal hit parade that you will enjoy working with.

• **A Side Trip - Sevenths**: To understand the nature and utility of 7th chords, let's begin by comparing how these 7th chords *sound* when they're played against their "non-7th" counterparts. We'll work with some of the chords we've already learned, specifically, **C**, **D**, **G**, and **A**. What I'm presenting below are mini-charts of the chords we've already covered that are set against a full-sized chart of the relevant 7th chord that you'll add to your chord inventory. The small inset boxes provide tips on forming these new seventh chords.

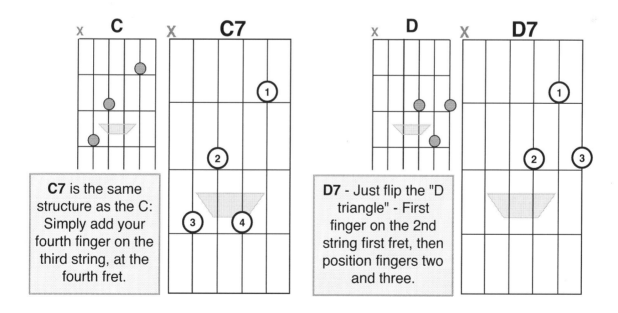

C7 is the same structure as the C: Simply add your fourth finger on the third string, at the fourth fret.

D7 - Just flip the "D triangle" - First finger on the 2nd string first fret, then position fingers two and three.

33

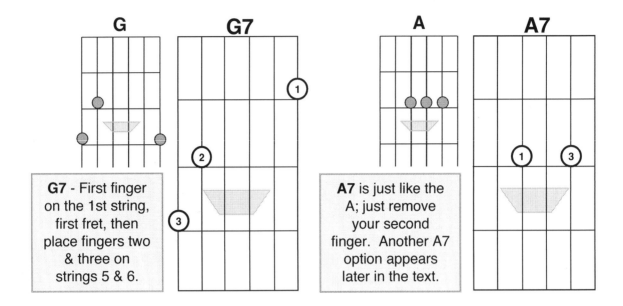

G7 - First finger on the 1st string, first fret, then place fingers two & three on strings 5 & 6.

A7 is just like the A; just remove your second finger. Another A7 option appears later in the text.

Having charted these four major chords and their "7th" counterparts, let me suggest three simple exercises that might prove helpful in getting a feel for how these 7th chords sound, how they stack up to other chords sequences, and how they relate to other progressions:

• **First**, once you get the hang of the new 7th chords, try playing them in reference to the major chords as mentioned above. Strum the C chord four times then move to the C7 for four strums and repeat this routine with the D, G, and A chords. Take your time and try to move from the major chord to the 7th chord in a steady rhythm. Concentrate on how the 7th sounds in relation to the major. You'll hear a subtle difference between the two. To me, when I go from a C to a C7, it often sounds like the C7 *is anticipating another chord*. It's as if the C7 expects me to move to the next harmonically compatible chord. This is *one* of the key functions of 7th chords. They are sometimes called "passing" chords because they set up an audio avenue from one chord to the next chord. This suggests the next exercise on the following page.

• **Second**, let's try to inject some 7th chords into a song we've already studied, "Amazing Grace." The original chords appear in a bold font (**C**) and the 7th chords appear in an outline font (C7). I'm adding **7th** chords to the original structure to present examples of "passing chords." In the first line, I've introduced the **C7** after three **C** strums (or beats). I'm hoping that you'll notice that these three **C7** strums *suggest* the next chord, an **F** chord. Similarly, the **G7** is used in the third line after three **G** strums as a *suggestion* for the forthcoming **C** chord that begins the third line. I've also replaced the **G** in the fourth line with **G7** to *suggest* the final chord of the last line which is a **C** chord.

```
C              C7          F           C
A - mazing    Grace, how sweet the   sound, that
 /  /  /  /  /  /  /  /  /  /  /  /

C              C7          G           G7
Saved     a   wretch   like me.              I
 /  /  /  /  /  /  /  /  /  /  /  /

C              C7          F           C
once      was lost,      but  now   I'm found, was
 /  /  /  /  /  /  /  /  /  /  /  /

C              G7          C
Blind,        but  now        I   see.
 /  /  /  /  /  /  /  /  /  /  /  /
```

• **Third**, we will create a sequence that features 7th chords and their contextual *flavor* in a song-like setting. In other words, we'll create a little "riff" that shows how these particular chords can contribute to the *sound* and *feel* of a particular piece of music. In mentioning a "riff," I'm talking about a term that contemporary musicians commonly use to identify a short segment of notes or chords that create a recognizable sound or a familiar harmonic sequence. An example of a note-oriented riff might be the hard-driving single notes that kick off the song, "(I Can't Get No) Satisfaction," and an example of a chord-oriented riff might be the continuous cycle of the E, D and A chords that define the rock classic, "Gloria."

To develop a riff that illustrates the utility of 7th chords, we'll create our own D Progression and use several of the chords we've just learned, specifically, the D7, G7, and A7. Before laying out this 7th-oriented riff in D, I'd like to introduce an alternative way to play the A7 chord.

This new version is very much like the original A chord we previously learned, we're just adding another note to the higher register of the chord to make it a 7th chord. Instead of squeezing your first three fingers into the cramped space that you did in the original A configuration, just lay down your first finger and depress all three notes on strings 2, 3, and 4 at the second fret. It doesn't matter if you interfere with the first string in this effort because you'll be placing your third finger on the 1st string at the third fret. To my ear, this version of the A7 chord seems to highlight the "7th" sound of the chord. Try playing the previous version of the A7 that just required your first and third fingers then try this version. I think you'll find that this version seems to deliver more of a "7th edge."

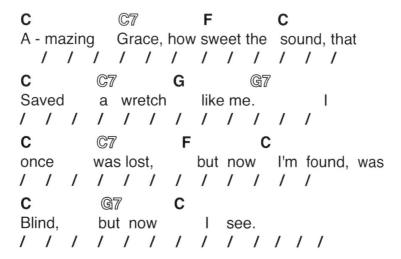

A7

In creating our "7th-oriented D riff" we're using the same techniques we used in playing songs like "Amazing Grace" and "Happy Birthday." We're using the three primary chords of a particular progression. In this case, we're using the D Progression whose primary chords are the D, G, and A. We're simply turning several of these chords into 7th chords to illustrate how these chords sound and feel when they're used together. Our "D Riff" features two sixteen-beat lines. Here are the charted versions of the two lines you will be working with:

D   **D7**   **G7**   **D**   **D7**   **A7**
/ / / / / / / / / / / / / / / /

D   **D7**   **G7**   **D**   **A7**   **D**
/ / / / / / / / / / / / / / / /

We'll start slowly by taking it one line at a time. For the **first line** begin with two strums on the D chord, then two strums in D7. Move on to four strums on the G7, two on the D, two on the D7, and finish the line with four strums on the first version of the A7 chord. This is the version that requires using your first and third fingers on the second fret as pictured to the right. To my ear, ending the first line with the A7 creates the *audio suggestion* that you will be returning to the original D chord. The **second line** is the same as the first for the initial ten beats or strums. It finishes with a bit of a flourish that creates a feeling of continuity between the two lines. In other words, the two lines played together sound like a logical sequence of chords or a segment of a song. One of the elements for this so-called flourish at the end of the second line is the underscored A7. I've underlined this A7 to indicate that you should play the second version of the chord as it appears in the A7 chart to the right. I think you will agree that this newer version of the A7 chord seems to have more seventh-sounding bite than the initial version. This prominent seventh sound is the product of the note that distinguishes the seventh chord, the G note. In the newer A7 configuration, the G is situated at the top of the chord in the higher register at the third fret of the 1st string. The high-register G note cuts through with more of the 7th flavor.

Play these two lines over and over in a steady cycle. Settle into a tempo that is slow enough to allow you time to properly change chords. Your ability to switch from one chord to the next is a function of practice, so *please* keep at it.

· **Summing Up the Sevenths**: We began this "Side Trip of Sevenths" by comparing the sound and texture of the major chords against the sound and texture of the 7th chords. We then addressed the use of 7th chords as *passing chords*. The passing chords can be helpful in spicing up a bland progression or by lending a sophisticated feel to a standard chord sequence. Finally, we put a series of major and seventh chords to work through the "7th-Oriented D Riff." I hope that you can hear the delicate difference of textures in the D riff. Once you've gotten your chord changes down for the riff and once you've established a steady groove, try running through it without the 7th chords. You should be able to sense a notable audio shift. The riff simply *feels* different. To my ear, the 7th structure sounds more edgy. It sounds more like a rock song than a folk song. It sounds more like a classic blues number than a ballad.

        As you might expect there are many other examples of seventh chords. I will be introducing more of these chords as we move through the *Manual*.

        I fully realize that all this talk of "feels" and "textures" is very subjective, but I sincerely hope you can hear the subtle differences I'm trying to describe. Ultimately, you'll settle on your own set of terms to describe what you're hearing, and I'm confident that you will find these subtle variations helpful as you continue to explore new riffs and songs and begin to write your own material.

Key of F · Basic Chord Progression

In the world of modern pop music, from the mid-fifties to the present, the Key of F hasn't enjoyed the popularity of the other keys we've considered so far—the Keys of C, D and E. It's a key more commonly associated with earlier twentieth century styles that focused on horns, big bands, and orchestral arrangements. The standard F progression is a challenging progression to play on lower frets of the guitar. This is because two of the three primary chords, F and B♭, can be played conveniently only in a four-string format. The progression is much more accessible in a barre-chord format which we will address later in the *Manual*. Accordingly, we won't spend a great deal of time on it at this point. Nevertheless, you should be familiar with this progression in its minimal format. And, through the years, I've found that abbreviated versions of chords like the F and the B♭, come in handy in various performance situations.

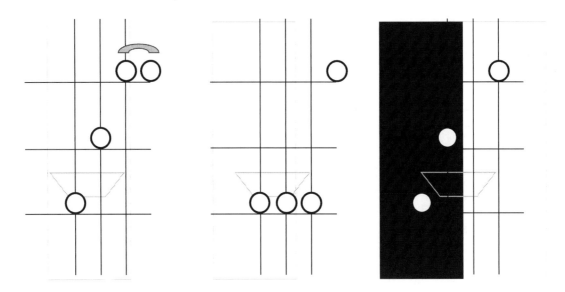

We've already addressed the F chord and the C chord but we've yet to address the B♭ chord. You might recall the B chord from the E Progression (see page 30). The B♭ is the same configuration played a half step (one fret) below the B chord. In other words, you "**flat**" the B chord a half step to create the B♭. Please notice that you don't play the 5th or the 6th string with this abbreviated version of the B♭ chord.

Finally, there's Dm, the relative minor chord for the Progression. Form the Dm chord by placing your first finger on the first fret of the 1st string and then extending your second finger to the second fret of the 3rd string. Finalize the chord by placing your third finger on the third fret of the 2nd string. Notice that the low E (6th) string is omitted.

X **Dm**

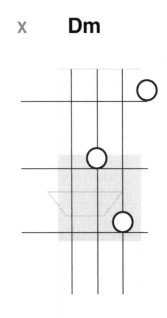

• **A Side Trip - Arpeggios**: According to my dog-eared *Webster's Ninth New Collegiate Dictionary*, an arpeggio refers to the "production of the tones of a chord in succession and not simultaneously." What that boils down to is picking out the various notes of a chord rather than strumming the entire chord. Let's take the F chord as an example.

      The four-string F chord begins on the 4th string and includes the 3rd, 2nd, and 1st strings. To create an arpeggio, you would pick the note on the 4th string (which is an F note), then the note on the 3rd string (which is an A note), then the note on the 2nd string (which is a C note), and finally the note on the 1st string (which is another F note one octave above the original F note of the chord). Technically, you could mix up the order in picking the four individual strings or you could start with the highest note and pick the single notes in reverse order. At this point though, we'll start on the lowest note and move to the highest note which is a very common form of an arpeggio. You can either play the individual notes with a pick, with your thumb, or, if you're feeling adventurous, you could "finger-pick" the notes.

      To "finger-pick" these four notes, play the 4th string with your thumb, then play the 3rd string with your first finger, the 2nd string with your second finger, and the 1st string with your third finger. Begin by striking the 4th string with a *downward* motion of your thumb and continue by plucking the three remaining strings with an *upward* movement of your individual fingers. Essentially, you "thumb down" on the first note of the arpeggio, and you "pinch up" with designated fingers to sound the three highest notes.

      We will include all four chords from the F Progression in the following arpeggio exercise: The F chord which is the Tonic or the I; the Dm which is the relative minor or the VIm; the Bb chord which is the Subdominant or the IV; and the C chord which is the Dominant or the V.

      If this finger-picking method is too troublesome, don't worry. Use the picking technique of your choice. Also, choose a relaxed tempo that you can maintain with confidence and try to keep the tempo steady as you move from note to note in each individual chord. It will take a little time to move from chord to chord, but don't be discouraged. Smoother transitions are simply a matter of time and effort. We will work on a steady overall time signature in the next exercise.

      Before beginning this exercise, let me mention that the F chord and the Bb chord are both "4-string chords." The Dm and the C however are "five-string" chords. Why aren't we playing all five notes of the "five-string" chords? The answer lies in keeping a balanced number of notes from chord to chord. It would be rather awkward to use four notes on one line and then try to squeeze five notes into the next line. It could be done, but it requires some "timing and meter" acrobatics that are neither convenient nor relevant at this point. Consequently, we'll keep it simple by playing four "arpeggiated" notes per chord. As a convenience, I'm providing charts of the four chords we'll be using.

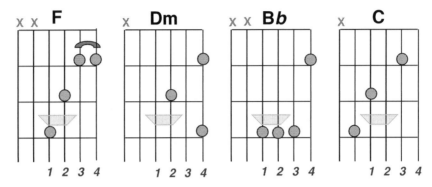

The numbers at the bottom of the individual chord charts indicate the strings to be played and their proper sequence in the "arpeggio." Slowly play the four notes of the F chord, reposition for the Dm chord, then play the four notes designated for that chord and move through the other two chords in a similar fashion.

• **Creating a Handy Little Song Riff**: In this new exercise, pick the four notes of the F chord as described above (moving from the 4th string through the 1st string) using whichever picking technique you're comfortable with. Play this configuration twice at a slow and steady pace.
• Move to the Dm chord and repeat the four-note picking structure you used on the F chord. Play this configuration twice.
• Move to the B♭ chord and repeat the same four-note picking structure and play this configuration twice.
• Move to the C chord and repeat the same four-note picking structure beginning on the 4th string and moving up to the 1st string. Once again, play this twice.
• Now pull the four chords together into a coherent "riff!" Begin on the F and run through all of the chords playing the single "arpeggio" notes as follows:

F Chord Notes:	/	/	/	/	/	/	/	/
	1	2	3	4	1	2	3	4
Dm Chord Notes:	/	/	/	/	/	/	/	/
	1	2	3	4	1	2	3	4
B♭ Chord Notes:	/	/	/	/	/	/	/	/
	1	2	3	4	1	2	3	4
C Chord Notes:	/	/	/	/	/	/	/	/
	1	2	3	4	1	2	3	4

• The primary challenge in this exercise is to keep your timing steady as you move from one chord to the next. A quick switch to the B*b* is a particularly difficult move but mastering chord changes is a product of practice so please hand in there!

When you start the exercise begin playing the structure at a pace that's slow enough to allow you to adequate time to change chords and continue in a constant groove. As you begin to develop a steady pace, you might notice that this riff sounds familiar. The chord sequence, F, Dm, B*b*, and C is the same *structure* as C, Am, F and G which is based on the first progression we learned. Both of these structures use the same primary chords and relative minors that apply to their respective progressions. Here is a brief review that illustrates the connection between the structures of different progressions:

KEY C	KEY F	This comparison is yet another example of transposing from one key to another. It also reinforces the common structures of all chord progressions.
C	**F**	Both chords are "I" chords or **Tonic** chords.
Am	**Dm**	Both chords are "VIm" or **Relative Minor** chords.
F	**B***b*	Both chords are "IV" chords or **Subdominant** chords.
G	**C**	Both chords are "V" chords or **Dominant** chords.

Although the single-note "arpeggio" style in the F exercise gives the F Progression a different feel, it's easy to hear that both of these chord sequences share a harmonic bond. With that in mind, let's try the arpeggio technique with the C, Am, F and G sequence. Applying this technique to the C Progression will allow us to stretch out a bit on our arpeggios. By "stretching out," I'm referring to playing more arpeggiated notes for each individual chord. With the C Progression, we're going to play **six** individual notes with each chord. We can do this without much difficulty because the C, Am and G are all five- or six-note chords. Only the F is a four-note chord. This exercise will take us into some new territory regarding playing arpeggios. In playing six arpeggiated notes in each chord, we'll start with the lower strings then move through the higher strings. From time to time however, if you are using a four-note or a five-note chord, you'll "run out of strings." At that point you must double back and play strings you've previously played to maintain the six-note balance for each chord. This is all made clear through the following exercise. We'll begin with chord charts for the C Progression that indicate the sequence and direction of the arpeggiated notes at the bottom of each chord chart.

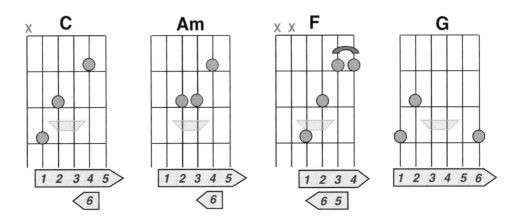

Once again, the numbers at the bottom of the chord charts indicate the individual strings and the sequence in which you will play them. I've added arrows pointing to the *right* to indicate notes that are played in an *ascending* order as well arrows pointing to the *left* to indicate notes that are played in a *descending* order. Notice that the numbers in the "descending" arrows are placed below the string that is to be played. With the Am chord, the sixth note is below the 2nd string, and with the F chord, the fifth and sixth notes are below the 2nd and 3rd strings. Each chord is to receive two sets of six notes. The initial six-note set appears in **regular** type and the second six-note set appears in *outline* type as indicated below:

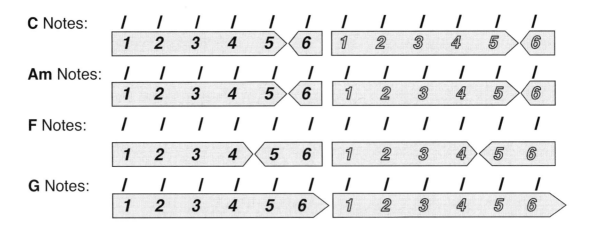

This configuration mirrors the "Handy Little Song Riff" exercise in F except we're using six arpeggiated notes per chord instead of four. As a follow up to this exercise, try playing only one 6-note set per chord. By cutting the length of the riff in half, you're creating a more challenging exercise by forcing quicker chord changes.

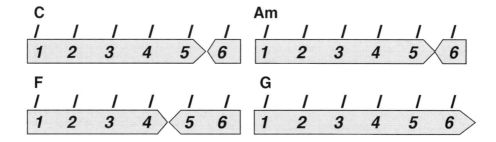

All of these arpeggiated sequences suggest the popular "Oldies Progression" that we discussed on pages 25 and 26. Just as a reminder, the "Oldies Progression" is the I (one chord), the VIm (the relative minor chord), the IV (four chord), and the V (five chord). In the examples above, this equates to the progressions of F - Dm - B♭ - C and C - Am - F - G. With only a slight rearrangement, these arpeggiated sequences also suggest the "Pop-Punk Chord Progression" that features the sequence of the I (one chord), the V (five chord), the VIm (the relative minor chord), and the IV (four chord). In the examples above, this equates to the progressions of F - C - Dm - B♭ and C - G - Am - F. I suggest that you revisit our discussion on **"Some 'Historical' Thoughts on the C-Am-F-G Progression"** on page 25 to explore some of the song possibilities connected with that apply to these progressions. As a worthwhile exercise, you can try to play certain songs in an arpeggiated format rather than a strumming format. Ultimately, as we move through more progressions and as we move through the barre chords, you can try the arpeggio techniques on an entirely new collection of chords.

Key of G · Basic Chord Progression

The G Progression is one of the most popular and most widely used progressions in American popular music. A great deal of the progression's popularity is linked to the tremendous popularity of the guitar after WWII. Beyond any doubt, the guitar and its early predecessors have been around for quite a while—more than a thousand years according to most music historians—but the instrument's "cool factor" exploded with the birth of rock 'n' roll and related pop music genres in the 1950s and 1960s. Before rock 'n' roll became the big new thing, the swing bands, orchestras, and multi-instrument ensembles enjoyed the spotlight in American pop culture with brass, woodwinds and other horns of all shapes and sizes as the primary instruments of choice. These "orchestra" instruments are configured and tuned much differently than the guitar and many of the songs and musical scores are packed with sharps, flats, and keys that favored horn and orchestral arrangements rather than guitar arrangements. When rock 'n' roll hit the streets, the songs and music scores reflected more guitar-friendly keys like C, G, E, A, and D rather than more challenging keys like Ab, Bb, Eb, and F. The G Progression is one of several progressions that became quite popular in the rock, country, folk, and pop-music world. This is not to say that these progressions were not popular before. Blues players have used these basic progressions since the mid-nineteenth century, folk artists like Woody Guthrie and Pete Seeger relied on them, bluegrass players who helped set the stage for modern country music embraced these simple structures as did country pioneers like Jimmie Rodgers and Hank Williams in the pre-rock days. But when Elvis and the rockers permeated the airwaves, the movie theaters, the television sets, and the high school auditoriums across the country, a young baby-boomer generation with the disposable income and the desire to buy records   t tickets welc   ' ''   ɹitar as the ɕ ' · ·   ɘnt of choice! Here ar   y chords for   ession:

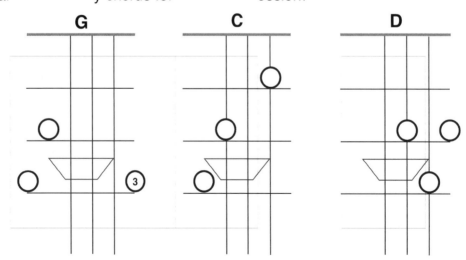

These are all familiar chords we have addressed before. In this progression, G is the "I" chord or the "Tonic," C is the "IV" chord or the "Subdominant," and D is the "V" chord or "Dominant." The relative minor, "VIm," for this progression is Em which is charted to the right. The Em is very similar to the E Major chord. You simply remove your first finger from the 3rd string at the first fret to create the Em chord. All of these chords are relatively easy to play, so run through the progression a few times by playing G for a few strums, then on to Em, C and D. This is the "Oldies Progression." You might also try to mix up the progression by playing four strums on the G, then four on the D, followed by four strums on the Em, and finally four strums on the C chord. This is the "Pop-Punk Chord Progression." Any of the songs you have tried in the Key of C, D, E or F, easily apply to the Key of G. In other words, you can transpose songs previously played in other keys to the Key of G.

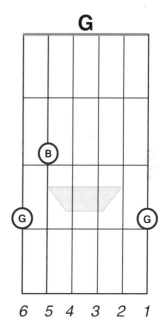

• **A Side Trip - Pick & Strum (P&S)**: This side trip takes us down a new road. We are going to explore new ways to strum chords. Specifically, we are going to focus on a technique that involves picking certain bass notes of a chord and then strumming the chord. We will begin with the G chord. The chart to the right lays out a standard G chord, and the numbers at the bottom of the chart show the individual strings. Notice however, that instead of designating which fingers you use in forming the chord, I am showing the actual notes that those specific finger positions create. In other words, by placing your second finger on the third fret of the 6th string, you are playing a **G** note, by placing your first finger on the second fret of the 5th string you are playing a **B** note, and by placing your third finger on the third fret of the 1st string you are playing a **G** note in a higher octave.

We will begin this exercise with a fundamental pick and strum (P&S) move by plucking the G note on the 6th string then strumming the chord. Use your pick to strike the G and then quickly strum the entire chord. This is best accomplished by setting the P&S move to a slow, steady beat. We will use an example that we are all familiar with, the "Alphabet Song." We have all sung that familiar tune, "A, B, C, D, E, F, G . . . " In this case, we will only use the first line

of the song to illustrate the basic P&S move. Also, in this brief exercise, we will
put the word "and" between the letters: "A-and, B-and, C-and, D-and, etc.
Starting with a slow but steady tempo, hit your bass **G** note as you sing "A" and
strum the chord on the "and." Imagine that simple melody and its timing and play
G-strum, G-strum, G-strum, G-strum:

"A"   **"B"**   **"C"**   **"D"**

/   and   /   and   /   and   /   and

G • strum   **G** • strum   **G** • strum   **G** • strum

Repeat this passage a few times to get the gist of the P&S move. If you
miss a string or two in strumming the full G chord, don't worry. Creating a steady
and relaxed P&S technique is more important than striking all six strings of the
chord. This holds true for four-string or five-string chords. If you play the bass
note of a chord in a crisp and consistent fashion, it is OK to brush the majority of
the remaining strings. Just keep it steady and smooth. Let us now consider the
rest of the chords in the G Progression we will be using in the P&S mix:

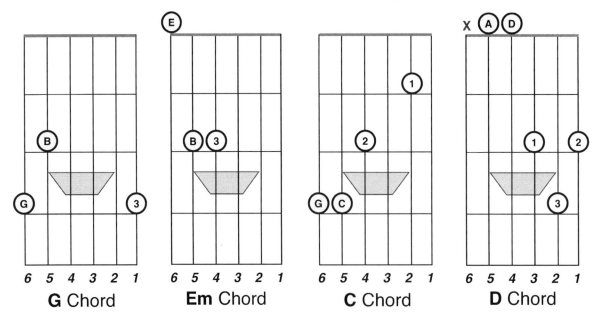

In the four chord charts above, I have highlighted the bass notes that will be used
in our P&S exercise with a gray background overlaid with the name of the note,
(Ⓖ for example). I am sure that by now you know the proper fingers to use in
these shaded notes. The numbered, non-shaded circles (② for example),
represent the standard finger positions that do not factor into the bass note
structure. Also, please note the shaded note circles above certain open strings.
The Em chord features an open 6th string (Ⓔ) as a bass note, and the D chord
features two open-string bass notes, an A note on the 5th string (Ⓐ) and a D
note on the 4th string (Ⓓ). These open-string bass notes are important in the

forthcoming exercise. Finally, you might notice that the C chord **C** (Six String)
different from the standard C chord we have been using.
The new C chord isa six-string chord that is charted to the
right. The positions of your first finger and second finger are
the same as the standard five-string C chord. Your third finger
that would normally be on the 5th string at the third fret is
moved over to the 6th string at the third fret. Your fourth finger
now plays the note on the 5th string at the third fret that was
previously played by your third finger. The result is a full six-
string C chord. This new configuration allows you to play the
G note on the 6th string and the **C** note on the 5th string that
will be useful in the following P&S exercise.

- **Get to Know the Notes & Chords**: Before diving into a P&S exercise with the
entire G-Em-C-D sequence, take a moment to practice "picking and strumming"
the individual chords presented above. Try the G chord: Play the bottom G note
then strum the strings; play the B note then strum the strings. Try the Em: Play
the low E string then strum; play the B note on the 5th string then strum. Try the
C: Play the root C note on the 5th string then strum; play the bottom G note on
the 6th string then strum. Finally, try the D: Play the root D note on the open 4th
string then strum; play the low A note on the open 5th string then strum. As you
practice playing the bass notes in conjunction with the chords, notice that
sometimes the initial bass note you play will be on the lowest string of the chord
while at other times, it will be on a higher string. With the G and Em chords, the
initial bass note involves the 6th string, but with the C chord, the initial bass note
falls on the 5th string with the second note falling on the 6th string. With the D
chord, the first bass note falls on the 4th string and your second note falls on the
5th string.

      If you would rather use the original C chord instead of **C** (Five-String)
the six-string version for the P&S exercises, that is just fine.
Simply alternate your third fretting finger between the C note
(5th string @ third fret) and the G note (6th string @ third fret).
Strike the C note on the 5th string then strum, then move your
third finger over to the G note on the 6th string, strike, and
strum. You will find that by reaching over to the 6th string,
your third finger might touch the 5th string and mute it. The
muting of the 5th string is actually desirable in this situation.
The A note (the open 5th string) that you created when you
removed your third finger from the 5th string, does not belong
in the C chord. From time to time in playing various chords it
is necessary to mute certain notes. I realize I have preached

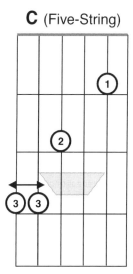

the practice that each note in a given chord should ring through clean and clear, but certain chords sometimes require subtle forms of string muting.

• **Pick & Strum with the Full G Progression**: The G-Em-C-D structure we are about to play is the same "I" chord + VIm (Relative Minor) + "IV" chord + "V" chord sequence we have addressed in several of our previous progressions. We are simply going to apply the pick and strum techniques you practiced in the "Get to Know the Notes & Chords" section on the previous page by framing them in a four-chord G Progression set to a rhythm pattern.

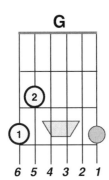

In the G chord diagram to the left, I have labeled the two bass notes as **1** and **2**. These numbers represent the *order in which these notes are played*. First, you will strike the 6th string on the third fret (which is a **G** note) then strum the chord just like we did in our previous exercises. Next, you will strike the 5th string on the second fret (which is a **B** note) and again strum the chord. You will then repeat the process and run through the cycle until you can develop a fluid pick and strum pattern. This P&S technique enables you to play an alternating bass line between the **G** note and the **B** note in sync with a steady strum. This is a very powerful accompaniment method in playing your songs, in playing with other players, and in mastering other guitar performance techniques.

We will now begin to integrate the rest of the G Progression chords into the mix. The important thing to notice in the charts below is the sequence of the alternating bass notes in the various chords. I have already commented on the G chord—strike the 6th string at third fret then strum and then strike the 5th string at second fret and strum. The same holds true for the Em chord—strike the open 6th string (an **E** note), then strum, then strike the 5th string - second fret (a **B** note) and strum. The alternating bass notes are different in the C and the D chords. With the C chord, strike the 5th string at third fret (a **C** note) then strum, then strike the 6th string at third fret (a **G** note) and strum. With the D chord, strike the open 4th string (a **D** note) then strum, then strike the open 5th string (an **A** note) and strum.

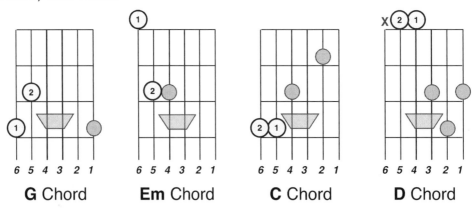

G Chord   **Em** Chord   **C** Chord   **D** Chord

Now take some time to practice these alternating bass notes on a chord-by-chord basis. Repeat these individual chords and their bass notes until you can play the Pick & Strum combination smoothly. You might find it helpful to set your tempo to the "Alphabet Song" we used earlier. In other words, just as you would sing "A and B and C and D" as a timing reference, you can use the same technique and plug in the appropriate bass note to be played as you sing along:

Sing Along: "G - strum - B - strum - G strum - B strum" for the sequence below:
    G Chord: 6th string (**G** note) + strum - 5th string (**B** note) + strum & repeat

Sing Along: "E - strum - B - strum - E strum - B strum" for the sequence below:
    Em Chord: 6th string (**E** note) + strum - 5th string (**B** note) + strum & repeat

Sing Along: "C - strum - G - strum - C strum - G strum" for the sequence below:
    C Chord: 5th string (**C** note) + strum - 6th string (**G** note) + strum & repeat

Sing Along: "D - strum - A - strum - D strum - A strum" for the sequence below:
    D Chord: 4th string (**D** note) + strum - 5th string (**A** note) + strum & repeat

Combining these four brief practice lines would look like this:

    G - strum - B - strum - G strum - B strum

    E - strum - B - strum - E strum - B strum

    C - strum - G - strum - C strum - G strum

    D - strum - A - strum - D strum - A strum

There is a reason I have altered the sequence of these alternating bass notes in the C and the D chords. In playing alternating bass lines, it is customary to strike the *root note* of chord *first* and to strike the accompanying bass note *second*. This practice establishes a sort of "audio continuity." By initially striking the root note, you are *suggesting* the nature of the chord that will follow. I have found that a predictable "audio continuity" is generally pleasing to most ears and to most audiences.[5] That said, there is nothing written in stone that says you must always start a P&S sequence with the root note . . . On down the line you might find it interesting to mix up these bass notes depending on the context of what you are playing and how it might contribute to the song at hand.

We will now pull these ideas together to create some coherent sequences using the basic chords of the G Progression. In the charts that follow, the smaller letters that appear before the chord designation represents the individual note that must be played before the chord is strummed. As an example, **G**/G means

---

[5] "Audio Continuity" and predictable chord and note patterns are generally welcomed by most listeners, but there is a definite appeal for the avant-garde, the dissonant, and the experimental. This of course is why the Guitar Gods invented jazz!

that you play the G bass note (6th string, 3rd fret), then strum the G chord, and **B**/G means that you strike the B bass note and then strum the G chord.

• **Sequence One: G-Em-C-D in 16 Beats**: The initial P&S sequence begins with four *"pick-strum"* beats of the G chord. To clarify exactly what I mean by a *"pick-strum"* **beat**, the first *"pick-strum"* **beat** ($^{G/G}_{/}$) requires picking the bass G note then quickly strumming the G chord, and the second *"pick-strum"* beat ($^{B/G}_{/}$) requires picking the bass B note then quickly strumming the G chord. Each so-called "beat" therefore, is a combination "pick-strum" move. After four *beats* in G, the sequence moves through four *beats* in Em, four in C, and four in D.

G/G	B/G	G/G	B/G	E/Em	B/Em	E/Em	B/Em
/	/	/	/	/	/	/	/
C/C	G/C	C/C	G/C	D/D	A/D	D/D	A/D
/	/	/	/	/	/	/	/

In running through this sequence, it might be helpful to think about the melodies of following songs: "Octopus's Garden" by the Beatles or "This Magic Moment" by the Drifters. The main, recognizable parts of these songs adhere to this basic structure. There are many, many melodies and song segments in pop music that channel the pattern above. For copyright reasons, I won't chart out the complete song with chords and lyrics, but if you look them up on the Internet, you will find a thorough treatment of these and many other tunes. In checking out these songs, check out the versions by different artists and try to find a version in the key you are working with. If you cannot find a version in the proper key, do not be discouraged. As we have learned, all of the progressions have the same structural characteristics. A structure or a sequence that works in the key of G will work in the key of A, B, C, D, E or F! If, for example, you search the Internet and find your song in the key of G, you can *transpose* those chords to the key of C. We touched on the idea of transposing chords from one key to another on page 29. In the G Progression exercise above, we are working with the I chord (G), the relative minor or the VI-minor chord (Em), the IV chord (C), and the V chord (D). To move your song from the Key of **G** to the Key of **C**, you simply plug in the I - VIm - IV - V chord sequence from the key of C. You should know from the first progression we studied—the C Progression on pages 20-22— that those chords are C-Am-F-G. To streamline the transposition process, I have provided a **Transposition Chart** on page 103 that will enable you to quickly move from one key to another. Using that chart, you can take the chords you find on the Internet and easily transpose them to the key of your choice.

• **Sequence Two: G-Em-C-D in Eight Beats**: In this eight-beat sequence, we are cutting the time we spend on each chord in half. You will stay on each chord for two beats which amounts to playing the first bass note and strumming then playing the second bass note and strumming. Begin with the G chord, strike the G note, strum, strike the B note, strum, move immediately to the Em chord, repeat the pick & strum move, then follow through the sequence with the C and D chords.

G/G	B/G	E/Em	B/Em	C/C	G/C	D/D	A/D
/	/	/	/	/	/	/	/

This sequence processes four chords in eight beats whereas the previous sequence processed the same four chords in sixteen beats. This "quickening" of the G Progression not only gives this four-chord progression a snappier feel, it opens the door to a number of song possibilities. Songs like Pete Seeger's folk mainstays like "Where Have All the Flowers Gone" and "If I Had a Hammer," or the 1961 pop classic, "Blue Moon," by The Marcels, are examples of this sequence in action. There is one song in the eight-beat P&S format that I would like to single out as a special example. The song, "Last Kiss," is one of the world's biggest pop-music tearjerkers. I single out this song because it has been a big hit for two different generations.

A flamboyant rockabilly artist named Wayne Cochran wrote the song in 1961 and released it on the small Gala label but it generated no significant chart activity. In 1964, the rock combo, J. Frank Wilson and the Cavaliers from San Angelo, Texas re-recorded the song and it blasted up the charts to #2 on the *Billboard Hot 100*. "Last Kiss" was one of several "teen tragedy songs" popular during the early rock 'n' roll era. Thirty-four years later, the Seattle-based rock band, Pearl Jam, recorded and released the same tune. Just like its predecessor, the Pearl Jam version reached #2 on the *Billboard Hot 100*. Consequently, the baby-boomers who recall the tune from 1964 and the young rock fans who initially heard the tune in 1996 share a common reference. Further, "Last Kiss" illustrates the staying power of a simple progression. The version by J. Frank Wilson and the Cavaliers is in the Key of E (E-D*b*m-A-B) and the version by Pearl Jam, which is remarkably similar to the original, is in the Key of G. The later version provides an excellent opportunity to play along in G, the key we are currently working with. The music video of the Pearl Jam version can be found at the website listed below and the chords and lyrics can be found at other locations on the Internet.

http://www.youtube.com/watch?v=uvjTo-hRD5c

• **Sequence Three: G-D-Em-C in Sixteen Beats**: We have worked with this sequence previously in studying variations on the C Progression on page 26. I mentioned that it was often called the "Pop-Punk Chord Progression" and that it was structurally different from the "1950s Progression" or the "Oldies Progression" which is the format we used above in the previous two P&S exercises. As you know, the "Oldies Progression" is a I - VIm - IV - V sequence, and the so-called "Pop-Punk Chord Progression" is a I - V - VIm - IV sequence. Let's see how this I - V - VIm - IV" progression unfolds in the sixteen-beat P&S exercise:

G/G	B/G	G/G	B/G	D/D	A/D	D/D	A/D
/	/	/	/	/	/	/	/

E/Em	B/Em	E/Em	B/Em	C/C	G/C	C/C	G/C
/	/	/	/	/	/	/	/

This exercise is similar to the original P&S sequence. The only difference is the order of the chords. Run through the changes until you can change chords effectively and maintain a steady rhythm in picking the individual bass notes.

We will now put these chords to work in a familiar setting by imagining it is New Year's Eve. "Auld Lang Syne" is a melody that most of us recognize even if we are not quite sure what the lyrics mean! From a late eighteenth-century poem by Scottish poet Robert Burns, "Auld Lang Syne" roughly translates as "for the sake of old times" and taken as a whole, the song is an invitation to let bygones be bygones. Like so many songs that are part of our shared cultural history, there are many ways to play this New Year's classic. I have based the following chart on the I-VIm-IV-V structure. This arrangement does not precisely *mirror* the sixteen-bar structure above. There are several places where the chords change more quickly, but it is very similar to the sixteen-bar exercise. Also, in charting the song, I have tried to stretch out the lyrics so they relate to the rhythm and the chord changes. This version of "Auld Lang Syne" is designed to be played slowly to allow adequate time for alternating bass notes and for moving smoothly from one chord to the next.

Auld Lang Syne

Should auld acquaintance be forgot
And never brought to mind
Should auld acquaintance be forgot
And days of auld lang syne
For auld lang syne, my dear,
For auld lang syne.
We'll take a cup o' kindness yet,
For auld lang syne.

An interesting side note: To consider that an Old-World classic like "Auld Lang Syne" and later 20th-century rock hits like the Rolling Stones' "Beast of Burden" and Journey's "Don't Stop Believing" share the same fundamental chord structure is a fascinating testimony to the structural similarities *and* the stylistic differences that characterize the unique interpretations over time of the fundamental twelve tones that define the DNA of Western music.

Auld Lang Syne

Count: *Should*

/   /   /   /

G/G	B/G	G/G	B/G	D/D	A/D	D/D	A/D
a u l d		*aquain - tance*		*b e*		*f o r g o t*	*and*

/ / / / / / / /

E/Em	B/Em	E/Em	B/Em	C/C	G/C	C/C	G/C
N e - v e r		*brought to*		*m i n d*			*Should*

/ / / / / / / /

G/G	B/G	G/G	B/G	D/D	A/D	D/D	A/D
a u l d		*aquain - tance*		*b e*		*f o r g o t*	*and*

/ / / / / / / /

E/Em	B/Em	C/C	D/D	G/G	C/G	G/G	C/G
Days	*of*	*auld*	*lang*	*syne*			*For*

/ / / / / / / /

G/G	B/G	G/G	B/G	D/D	A/D	D/D	A/D
a u l d		*l a n g*		*s y n e*	*my*	*d e a r*	*For*

/ / / / / / / /

G/G	B/G	G/G	B/G	C/C	G/C	C/C	G/C
a u l d		*l a n g*		*s y n e*			*We'll*

/ / / / / / / /

G/G	B/G	G/G	B/G	D/D	A/D	D/D	A/D
t a k e	*a*	*c u p*	*o f*	*k i n d n e s s*		*y e t*	*For*

/ / / / / / / /

E/Em	B/Em	C/C	D/D	G/G	C/G	G/G . . . *Let the G Chord Ring*
a u l d		*l a n g*		*s y n e*		

/ / / / / / /

As mentioned, I based the song chart above on the I-V-VIm-IV structure, but as you can see, it deviates from that structure during the course of the song. A slight modification of a basic chord sequence is a common occurrence in popular songs. If you have been referencing the Internet to find songs to use as examples for the progressions we have been discussing, you have probably discovered that the chorus or bridge of certain songs often deviates from the basic sequence. Such is the nature of songwriting. Still, there are many tunes that follow the standard progression formats we have been considering. Either way, learning the basic chord progressions is an invaluable tool in mastering your instrument. This brings us to the last adventure in the G Progression.

• **A Rockin' Internet Adventure**: I would like to refer once again to the I-V-VIm-IV structure that has been labeled the "Pop-Punk Chord Progression." As mentioned, this sequence would shake out as G - D - Em - C, in the Key of G. But, as you know, you can apply the I-V-VIm-IV sequence to any key. I bring this up because in the course of writing this *Manual*, I discovered that the I-V-VIm-IV sequence is a *much bigger deal* than I had previously realized. In checking out the pop charts of the late 60s, 70s, 80s, and 90s, I found that this progression is all over the place! Once I realized how popular this "Pop-Punk Chord Progression" was, I knew that I had more homework to do. We have already considered a few highly popular examples of the progression like "Beast of Burden" by the Rolling Stones, "Don't Stop Believing" by Journey, and "Let It Be" by the Beatles. In snooping around the Internet, I found a You Tube video that brings home the significance of this high-profile sequence. It is a live concert by a British group called the "Axis of Awesome." This video not only demonstrates that there are a tremendous number of major hits based on the I-V-VIm-IV sequence, but it also offers a great selection of newer songs, songs that I am not particularly familiar with, songs that will be helpful to many of our younger guitar players. Check out the following website and see if you do not agree:

http://www.youtube.com/watch?v=Co9mW_9hH2g&feature=related

After reviewing this video several times, I am convinced that the term "Pop-Punk Chord Progression" is not an accurate description of this sequence. I am sure that there are a number of Punk songs based on this progression, but the majority of the songs that I identify with this sequence are mainline pop and rock songs. If the "Oldies Progression" (I-VIm-IV-V) was front and center during the 1950s and early 1960s, the I-V-VIm-IV sequence has certainly eclipsed this early rock 'n' roll progression in the later part of the 20th century and maintains a strong presence through the second decade of the 21st century. With all of this in mind, I think it is time for a new name for this hot little chord sequence. From now on, we will call it the "Post-Oldies Progression," or the "**POP**" progression for short!

Key of A · Basic Chord Progression

The A Progression, like the E Progression, is well represented in the world of rock 'n' roll and pop music. There are countless tunes with R&B and blues-based flavors rooted in the A Progression. Similarly, there are folk songs, bluegrass songs, western swing & country tunes, and songs of all types and stripes in the Key of A. As a lead guitar player, I love the key of A. A great deal of the "A-based" lead-guitar activity is rooted in the middle reaches of the fretboard which allows me to scamper up and down the neck to incorporate different positions and "voicings" that are not readily available in other keys. I will address the notion of "voicings" when we consider the B Progression in the next segment, so please stand by. Further, there are certain tunes that just do not sound right unless they are played in the Key of A. Many of the guitar instrumental hits of the 1960s that I learned to play as a young guitar pup like "Walk Don't Run" or "Apache" are in the key of A. I mention "Walk Don't Run" for personal reasons. This instrumental classic recorded by the Seattle-based instrumental band "The Ventures" in 1960, truly caught my attention. Motivated by the terrific twang of the lead guitar I soon transformed from a skinny 6th-grade proto-nerd into a cool-cat, guitar-playing wannabe. Over 50 years later, I am still not sure whether or not I succeeded in my "wannabe" quest, but I am sure about the following chords that make up the fundamental A Chord Progression:

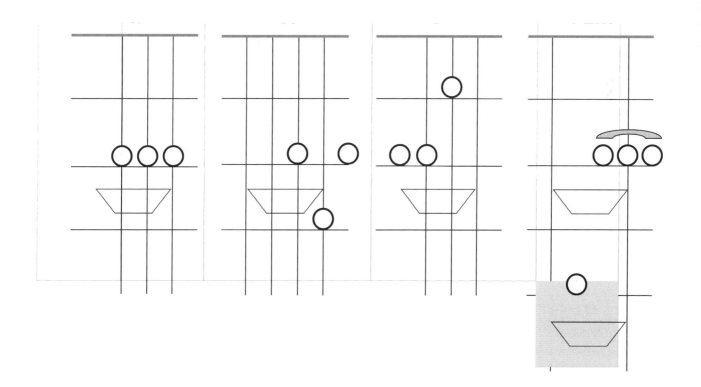

The three primary chords in this progression are all old friends. A is the "I" chord or the "Tonic," D is the "IV" chord or the "Subdominant," and E is the "V" chord or "Dominant." The newcomer is F#m, which is the "VI-minor" or relative minor. Once again, we are using an abbreviated four-string chord for the relative minor chord. To play the F#m, use your first finger to depress the 1st, 2nd, and 3rd strings at the second fret. To do this effectively, place your first finger on the strings then roll it back on its axis toward the headstock. This exposes the boney side of your finger which is more effective in depressing the strings. With your third finger, reach out to the 4th string at the fourth fret to play that note (an F#-Gb note). Avoid playing the 5th and 6th strings and you have an abbreviated F#m chord.

A7

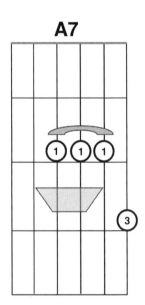

- **An Alternative Way to Play the A Chord**: We have been playing the A chord with fingers one, two, and three of the fretting hand as charted above. This technique works quite well for most applications of the chord. There is another way to approach the A chord using only one finger (see: bottom right). You can use your first finger to depress all the notes necessary to create the chord. I mentioned this "single-finger" technique when we worked on seventh chords as a Side Trip in the E Progression section. On page 36, I charted an A7 chord that required using your first finger to play the notes necessary for the basic A chord with the addition of the third finger on the third fret of the 1st string which provided the note needed to create the A7 chord. I have reproduced the A7 chart to the right.

A

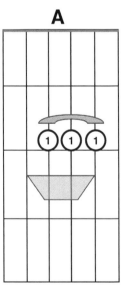

The Alternative A chord requires the same basic use of the first finger without the added "7th note." It looks simple enough on paper, but it can be a challenge physically. In using your first finger to play the A7 chord, it did not matter if you interfered with the 1st string because you would be playing the 1st string at the third fret. The alternative single-finger A chord requires that the 1st string rings through clean and clear. It cannot be muted by letting your first finger touch the 1st string. That means you have to arch your first finger *back* at the first knuckle to ensure that you do not interfere with the 1st string. This is a tight squeeze but give it a go and see if you can depress the three key strings at the second fret without muting the 1st string.

So why even bother with this "Alternative A chord?" There are several reasons: First, it is a physical exercise that will help you develop strength and dexterity in your first finger. This will come in handy when you begin playing barre chords which will require you to use your first finger as a "barre" to hold down all six strings. Second, the single-finger A chord can act as a "mini-barre." By holding down three strings with your first finger, you still have three other fingers available to play other notes and create other harmonic structures above the placement of your first finger. The chart to the left (**A/D**) illustrates the use of your second and third fingers in that capacity.

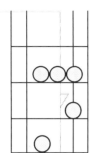

this structure by situating your first finger on the second fret as a mini-barre *but* avoid muting the first string. Then, place your second finger at the third fret of the 2nd string and your third finger at the fourth fret of the 4th string. This combination of the mini-barre and the additional two notes is a hybrid chord that is part A chord and part D chord. To get a feel for how this unique structure works, try a couple of strums with the single-finger A chord then add your 2nd and 3rd fingers as shown for a few more strums. Try a single strum of the single-finger A position followed by a single strum with fingers two and three in place. Begin rocking back and forth between these two positions. If you play these alternat'

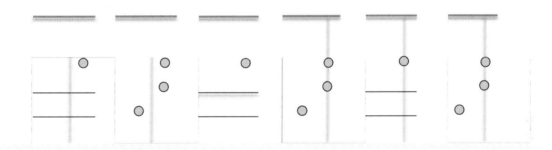

These charts represent the "rocking back and forth" move that I suggested above. Play the straight A, then add fingers two and three, play the A again, add fingers one and two and so forth. You can strum each "frame" one, two, or as many times you like, then strum the next "frame" the same number of strokes, or you can experiment and mix things up. It is important however, to maintain a steady rhythm as you move from frame to frame. This is one example of many such structures that can be used up and down the neck for a variety of chords, sounds, and textures. This will come into sharper focus when we address the barre chords in Chapter Four.

The third reason to consider this alternative A chord is to explore different finger positions in playing different chords. In the world of modern guitar playing, I do not believe that there is an ultimate "right" way or "wrong" way to approach a particular chord structure. Although many esteemed instructors might disagree, I would argue that unorthodox approaches and ad hoc techniques have produced an abundance of extremely successful guitar styles and popular compositions. Indeed, a quirky way to play a particular chord might yield a unique sound or a texture that ends up on the pop charts!

• **A Side Trip - Suspended Chords**: Do you remember the opening chords of "Pinball Wizard" by the Who or "Feel a Whole Lot Better" by the Byrds? How about something a little more recent like "Free Fallin'" by Tom Petty? These are all songs that feature a suspended fourth chord as the signature chord in the arrangement. From a *technical* perspective, a suspended fourth or "sus4" is a chord that omits the third and substitutes a perfect fourth note to complete the seminal chord triad. This fancy definition essentially means that you toss out one of the main notes of a particular chord and plug in another. In the case of an A chord, you would omit the C#-D♭ note and substitute the next highest note on the scale note which would be a D note. This modification of the A to the Asus4 is illustrated below.

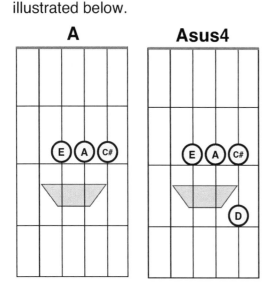

We will explore the theories, the rules, and the mechanics of creating sus4 and other chords in the *Matrix Method* chapter. We will do it in a way that does not rely on the complicated and often intimidating jargon commonly associated with standard notation. ("Standard notation" or "standard musical notation" is any system that represents music with written symbols, and in Western music, that means a five-line staff and notes.) The *Matrix Method* demystifies explanations like the following: "A 'sus4' is a chord that omits the third and substitutes a perfect fourth note to complete the seminal chord triad."

From an *audio* perspective, an Asus4 sounds pleasantly different from the regular A chord. There are historical and structural reasons why these chords are referred to as "suspended" chords—it has to do with carrying over a particular note from one chord to the next—but to my literary and guitar-playing ear, the word "suspended" suggests that a "sus4" chord leaves the listener in a state of mild auditory "suspense." That is, it leaves the listener with the feeling that something needs to happen in the musical sequence to *resolve* the perceived auditory suspension. As an example of how this sounds, imagine the hymns that people regularly sing in Christian church services. At the end of a hymn, the congregation sings a hearty "Amen" whereby the "A" part of "A-men" hangs in the air ("*Ahhhhhhhh*") and the "*men*" part *resolves* back to the main chord of the hymn. After the sound of "*men*" fades and the church falls silent, you can hear the gentle slap of the hymnals closing. Everyone knows the song is over. Not surprisingly, the "Ahhhhh" part of the closing chord sequence is a sus4 chord, and the "*men*" part of the chord sequence is the final major chord of the hymn which is the "resolved" version of the sus4 chord. In the case of our example in A above, an Asus4 would support the "*Ahhhh*," and the simple A chord would support the "*men.*" This is not to say the sus4 chords are only designed to put the finishing touches on songs—although they can and often do. This is to point out that the sus4 chords create a mild audio suspense followed by a harmonic resolution. We will now explore some other suspended chords, put them to work, and see what else they can do.

    All of the main chords of the A Progression—A, the I chord; D, the IV chord; and E, the V chord—are easily transformed into sus4 chords. The chord charts below illustrate the basic major chords and their sus4 cousins:

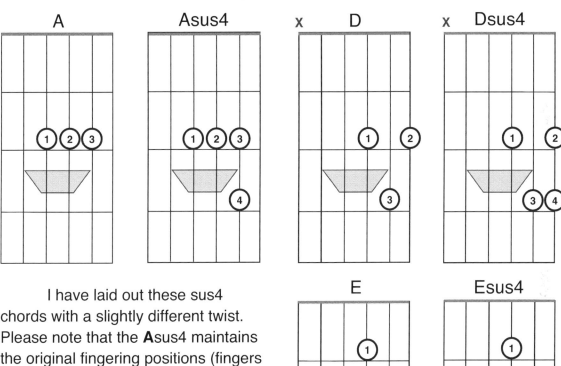

    I have laid out these sus4 chords with a slightly different twist. Please note that the **A**sus4 maintains the original fingering positions (fingers one, two and three on the second fret) even *after* you have added the fourth finger to complete the sus4 chord. The same holds true for the **D**sus4 and the **E**sus4 chords. By maintaining the original positions after you have added your fourth finger you can move back and forth from the root chord to the sus4 chord with minimal effort. This is

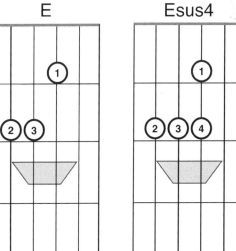

a trick that will come in handy on down the road. This simple placement of the fourth finger does not apply to all sus4 chords, but it certainly applies to Asus4, the Dsus4, and the Esus4. Now try these sus4 chords in a coherent sequence. This exercise works well in an upbeat tempo:

A   Asus4   A   Asus4   D   Dsus4   D   Dsus4
/   /   /   /   /   /   /   /   /   /   /   /   /   /   /   /

E   Esus4   E   Esus4   A   Asus4   E   Esus4
/   /   /   /   /   /   /   /   /   /   /   /   /   /   /   /

> The arrow at the end of the sequence indicates that you should return to the beginning of the exercise and repeat it. Keep repeating the sequence until your changes are steady and smooth.

We will now bring two new suspended chords into the mix, the Asus2 and Dsus2. Suspended *second* chords are common fare in popular music often used in conjunction with the sus4 chords. From a *technical* perspective, a suspended second is a chord that omits the third and substitutes a major second note to complete the seminal chord triad. (Again, more on this technical jargon in the *Matrix Method*.) From an *audio* perspective, the sus2 chord creates the "unresolved" feel much like the sus4 chord. Here are the Asus2 and the Dsus2 chords charted beside their derivative major chords.

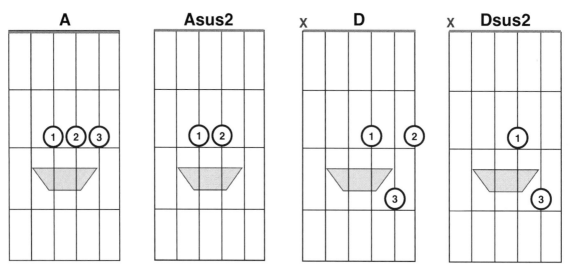

I hope that you can hear same "openness" in the sus2 chords that you heard in the sus4 chords. It is precisely this openness that sounds so pleasing when the sus2 and sus4 chords are played in conjunction with their supporting major chords. The following mini-charts represent those chord combinations.

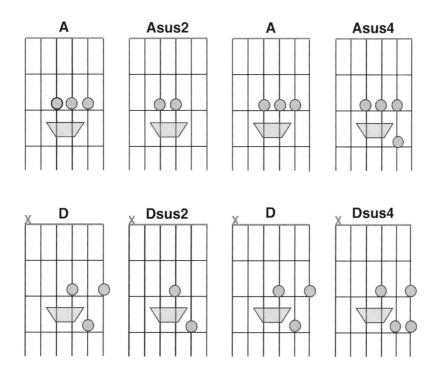

The following exercise reflects the chord sequence depicted above. By moving from the major to the sus2, then back to the major and on to the sus4 this exercise demonstrates a subtle melody. Play these chords at a slow, relaxed pace:

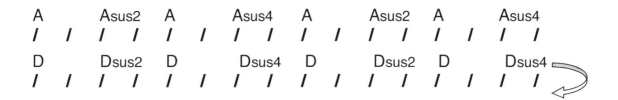

Having introduced the Asus2 and the Dsus2, you might ask, "What about the next logical chord in the sequence, namely, the Esus2?" There definitely *is* an Esus2 chord just as there is an Fsus2, an F#sus2 or G*b*sus2, a Gsus2 and so on, but it would be very difficult to properly fret an Esus2 in the first position on the lower frets. The barre chord system in Chapter Four provides a much more accessible technique for playing sus2 chords. Still, the E chord and the Esus4 can make a very worthy contribution to our current exercise. Here is one final example of the sus2 and sus4 chords that include E or "five" (V) chord. By including an E and an Esus4, we can get a feel for how the suspended chords sound in a complete I - IV - V progression.

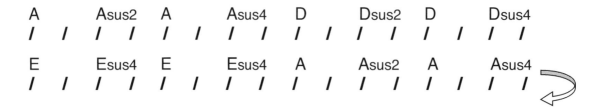

A	Asus2	A	Asus4	D	Dsus2	D	Dsus4
/ /	/ /	/ /	/ /	/ /	/ /	/ /	/ /

E	Esus4	E	Esus4	A	Asus2	A	Asus4
/ /	/ /	/ /	/ /	/ /	/ /	/ /	/ /

By playing these chords in a steady flow, you can hear a melodic theme or a recognizable riff that might remind you of certain songs you have heard on the charts. There are many popular music examples that highlight the use of suspended chords. The opening and verse section of "Pinball Wizard" by The Who is a series of suspended fourth chords. The iconic opening chord of "A Hard Day's Night" by The Beatles is a suspended chord, John & Yoko's Christmas song, "Happy Xmas (War Is Over)" is packed with suspended chords, and the signature lines of the Beatles' song, "I Need You" is an excellent example of the major to the sus2, then on to the sus4 and back to the major. Other high-profile suspended chord songs include rock classics like "Feel a Whole Lot Better" and "My Back Pages" by the Byrds. Again, I suggest you reference the Internet to find songs that embrace suspended chords that appeal to your musical tastes. There are countless examples in all genres. I also suggest mixing up the sequence of chords and experimenting with different tempos and rhythms. Because creating a sus4 or a sus2 chord from an A or a D chord is simply a matter of lifting up your 3rd finger and/or adding your 4th finger, you can have some fun with creating your own chord patterns. Take these colorful chords for a spin and see what you come up with!

Key of B · Basic Chord Progression

We won't spend a great deal of time on the B Progression because the relevant chords are difficult to play in the "first position." Once again, as a reminder, the first position, refers to chords played at the lower end of the fretboard, usually within the range of the first few frets. A first position chord stands in contrast to an advanced position chord formed higher up the neck. The signature chords of the progressions we've considered thus far—C, D, E, F, G, and A—have been relatively accessible in the first position. The primary chords of the B Progression (with the exception of the E chord) are more challenging will be presented as trimmed-down four-string chords.

The idea of a "first position" chord suggests another important term. That term is "voicing." To play a chord in the first position is to play a chord in a certain "voicing." To play that same chord in another position further up the neck is to play it another "voicing." When you play the standard C chord in the first position, you play the following five notes in the following order: C, E, G, C, and E. A variation of the same chord played higher on the neck might begin with a G note followed by C, G, C, E, and C. Still another variation even higher on the neck might begin with an E note followed by G, C, E, and C. Each of these variations or "voicings" present their individual notes in a different order. Additionally, each voicing sounds at a different pitch relative to its position on the fretboard. Although they are all C chords, each chord voicing produces a singular texture, sound, and feel.

· **Primary Chords of the B Progression**: The B chord is the I (tonic), E is the IV (subdominant), F# is the V (dominant), and Abm (or G#m) is the IVm (relative minor) for the progression.

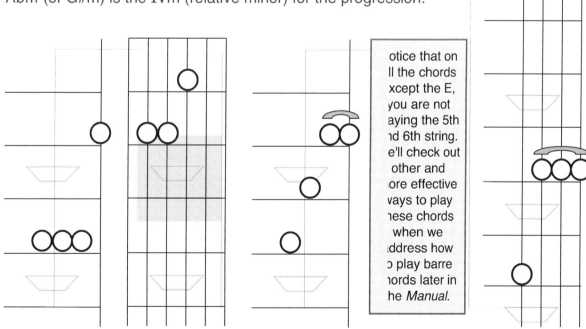

otice that on
ll the chords
xcept the E,
you are not
aying the 5th
ıd 6th string.
e'll check out
 other and
ore effective
vays to play
ıese chords
 when we
ıddress how
ɔ play barre
ıords later in
he *Manual*.

• **Playing through the B Progression** — The chords of this progression, B (I), Abm (VIm), E (IV), F# (V), present an excellent exercise for finger dexterity. Three of these chords are difficult to play and require special care to ensure that you strike only the designated strings. Beyond practicing these chords in the "Oldies Progression," consider mixing up the sequence to experiment with the "Post-Oldies Progression," or the "POP" progression — I, V, VIm, IV.

As a final thought on this progression and its relationship to barre chords. You will find the Key of B much easier to negotiate after we address the barre-chord techniques in Chapter Four. These techniques will not only highlight straightforward ways to play sharp and flat chords, they will provide the essentials you'll need to take on all the sharp and flat progressions ([F#-Gb] • [G#-Ab] • [A#-Bb] • [C#-Db] • [D#-Eb]) that we haven't covered yet.

• **A Side Trip - Time & Tempo**: Throughout this *Manual* I've talked about keeping time or maintaining a steady beat as you're playing the various exercises. I've tried to emphasize the importance of maintaining a steady tempo and a steady "groove." You've probably heard the old saying, "timing is everything." When it comes to playing music, particularly when you're playing with others, there's a great deal of truth in that classic phrase. Having played in bands for quite some time, I've found that it's a good idea for everyone to start and end a song at the same time and it *really* helps if everyone "counts to four" (or to "three" or to "two") the same way in between! Obviously, this is where time and tempo come in. First, let's consider some basic definitions and then assemble these various ideas into a straightforward system that will help you play in time, establish a "steady groove," and play "in the pocket!"

• **Definitions - Time & Tempo**: The notion of **Time** in music deals with the organization of *rhythm* through the passage of time and the grouping of *beats* into larger, regular patterns, notated as *measures* in simple *meters*. This rambling explanation requires some secondary definitions: The idea of **Rhythm** in music is characterized by repeating a sequence of stressed and unstressed beats divided into *bars* that are organized by *tempo* indications. A **Beat** is a basic unit of length in musical time. **Measure** refers to a rhythmic grouping or metrical unit that contains a fixed number of beats. **Meter** suggests the basic pulse and rhythm of a piece of music which is generally indicated in the number of beats there are in an individual measure. The musical term **Bar** is another word for **Measure**. **Tempo** is the rate of speed or the pace of a musical piece.

As you can see, all these definitions seem to depend on each other. They seem to be intertwined and sometimes blend into each other. In the initial definition of **Time** for example, we're introduced to the terms *rhythm, beat, measure, meter* as well as the word *time* as it relates to the common tick & tock of a clock and as it relates to music! If this were not confusing enough, the subsequent sentences of the definition introduce the terms *bar* and *tempo*. Allow me to chime in and offer my "workingman's" definition of musical time and tempo. Because music occurs on a timeline (as in the common tick & tock of a clock), each musical piece has a definite beginning, middle and end. And, because these melodic sounds have a rhythm and flow like a heartbeat, musicians need to agree on how they're going to count the rate and speed of that heartbeat. The aggregate of these agreements constitutes the generally acceptable principles of time and tempo, and these principles are commonly expressed in terms of **Time Signatures**.

Time signatures tell us what kind of beat & rhythm pattern to play in a particular song. Most people who enjoy listening to or playing music have heard terms like "four-four," "common time," and "three-quarter time," or "waltz time." These terms all indicate time signatures. If you examine a piece of sheet music, you'll find something like this in the upper left-hand corner at the beginning of the piece. The fraction, 4/4, depicts the time signature of the song. The numerator (the top figure) tells us that there are four beats in an individual measure and the denominator (the bottom figure) tells us the *time value* of those beats. By **time value** I'm referring to how long a particular beat lasts or how much room it occupies in a specific measure. I realize that the explanation about "time value" might sound a bit confusing, but I will address it in detail later on in the text. The numerator however is a clear-cut concept and reflects

The symbol to the left is a "Clef." It depicts the pitch range of the forthcoming notes. The four sharp (#) symbols indicate the key of the song. The four sharps tell us that the key is E because the basic E major scale has four sharp notes (E • F# • G# • A • B • C# • D# • E). The piggy-back fours to the right represent the fraction 4/4 which is the time signature. In this case that time signature is "four-four" or "common time."

ideas that we've used before. The illustration below is a remake of the beat charts we've used before in learning to play songs that show you when to strum the guitar. The forward slashes represent beats and the addition of the long rectangles represent the measures. The individual measures appear in a "light - dark" sequence to differentiate one measure from the next.

This chart represents four measures with four beats in each measure. Remember, the word "measure" and "bar" are interchangeable, so we could just as easily call this a four-bar sequence in common time or four-four time. Either way, it boils down to four beats per measure which is what the numerator in the time-signature fraction is telling us. Let's try counting out this 4/4 time signature in a practical setting by applying the lyrics of a familiar song to the beat structure. The first two lines of "Auld Lang Syne" will work quite well:

Should auld acquaintance be forgot and never brought to mind   Should

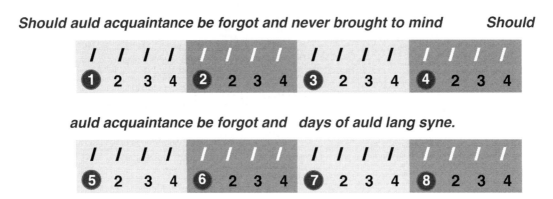

auld acquaintance be forgot and   days of auld lang syne.

The black numbered circles at the beginning of each measure indicate the progression of the individual measures. Try counting this out loud to get a feel for the timing of the piece: "*One, two, three, four; Two, two, three, four; Three, two, three, four; Four, two, three, four . . .*" By identifying each measure in a numbered sequence, musicians can communicate with each other about a specific point in a song. For example, one might say, "The bass doesn't kick in until the fifth bar." Or, "The sixth and seventh bars are in G, not in A like we were playing it yesterday." Bars are used to identify certain types of tunes. You have probably heard of a "twelve-bar" blues or a "twelve-bar" shuffle. A twelve-bar blues is a mainstay in the rock world and such structures abound at jam sessions, particularly a get-together with a covey of guitar players. Here's a little blues ditty I came up with for the occasion:

Woke up   this mornin' my baby   beat me with a broom

/	/	/	/	/	/	/	/	/	/	/	/	/	/	/	/
❶	2	3	4	❷	2	3	4	❸	2	3	4	❹	2	3	4

Woke up   this mornin' my baby   beat me with a broom   She said,

/	/	/	/	/	/	/	/	/	/	/	/	/	/	/	/
❺	2	3	4	❻	2	3	4	❼	2	3	4	❽	2	3	4

Get your butt a movin'   I got cleanin' to do!

/	/	/	/	/	/	/	/	/	/	/	/	/	/	/	/
❾	2	3	4	❿	2	3	4	⓫	2	3	4	⓬	2	3	4

This simple structure is the basic format for countless blues tunes as well as shuffles, which are faster, livelier renditions of this same format. And, as you can see, it boils down to twelve bars with four beats in each bar. This is the essence of the classic "twelve-bar blues."

We can use the same format to chart 3/4 time or, as it's often called "waltz time." We have the same four bars (measures) except we only have three beats in each bar. This of course, is exactly what the numerator (the top figure) in our fraction requires. It's telling us that there are three beats per measure. We'll consider the meaning of the denominator (the bottom figure) shortly.

Let's apply this 3/4 time signature to a familiar song. The small numbers in the upper left-hand corner of each measure is a simple "bar count." I include the bar count as a convenience and it has nothing to do with "real" musical notation:

A - mazing	Grace,	how sweet	the sound,	that
1 / / /	2 / / /	3 / / /	4 / / /	

Saved	a wretch	like me.		I
5 / / /	6 / / /	7 / / /	8 / / /	

once	was lost,	but now	I'm found,	was
9 / / /	10 / / /	11 / / /	12 / / /	

Blind,	but now	I see.		
13 / / /	14 / / /	15 / / /	16 / / /	

To count this sequence aloud, you would obviously count in "threes:" "*One, two, three; Two, two, three; Three, two, three,*" etc. To count through the entire verse, you would move through sixteen bars. Consequently, "Amazing Grace," is a sixteen-bar waltz.

These examples should give you a reasonable idea about one essential aspect of timing, explicitly, how the numerator works in our time signature fraction. There are many other time signatures like 5/4, 6/4, 7/4, 8/4, and the list goes on and on. An appreciable number of pop-music songs are either in 4/4 or 3/4 time. Further, what you've learned so far will enable you to read the basic chord charts that are used by many working musicians. Still, we haven't addressed the illusive denominator or lower figure in our fraction! All of the time signatures I've mentioned have "4" in the denominator and I'm uncomfortable with leaving this aspect unexplained *even* if it's not a fundamental factor into our practical, matrix-oriented model. Consequently, I'll explain how this denominator business works and to do that accurately, I must dabble in some *real* aspects of reading music.

We left our discussion about the denominator in the time signature fraction with this statement: "The denominator (the bottom figure) tells us the *time value* of [the beats within a specific measure]." I also mentioned that "By **time value** I'm referring to how long a particular beat lasts or how much room it occupies in that measure." In the enlightened world of reading and writing music, notes not only indicate a *tone* value but they also indicate a *time* value. The tone value— whether it's an A, B, C, D*b* or F# etc.—is indicated by the note's location on the

music staff. This illustration shows the various notes as they are situated on the staff. The lowest note on the lowest *line* is an E note and the highest note on the highest *line* is an F. The lowest note in the lowest *space* is an F note and the highest note in the highest *space* is E. The other notes are situated between these highs and lows as depicted to the left. This explains the tone value of notes, but what about their time value? How can these notes tell how long a certain tone should last? How can they tell you how much "space" they should occupy in an individual measure?

The answers to these questions are found in the shape of the note. Let's begin by identifying the various parts of a note. Each part of the note—the note

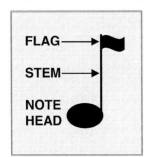

head, the stem and the flag—has a special role to play in communicating the time value of an individual note. In the example above, the notes on the staff don't have stems or flags. Each note is an oval with a hollow center, like a lopsided donut. These are whole notes and whole notes ring through an entire measure or bar. Put another way, if you're playing a song in 4/4 time with four

beats per bar, then a whole note would last through all four beats in that bar. Imagine this scenario: You're playing along to one of our Chord & Beat charts like "Auld Lang Syne," a song in 3/4 or waltz time. You're tapping your foot in time with the beat—one, two, three, one, two, three—and on each beat you're making a single strum on the guitar. As you play through the piece, you notice that a new measure requires a whole note rather than the usual three beats. Q: What do you do? A: You strike the chord on the first foot-tap (beat #1 of that measure) and let the chord ring as you tap through the last two beats of the measure. (Remember, we're in 3/4 time so there are three beats per measure). In other words, you give that whole note three-beats of space. If you were counting to yourself, it would sound like this: "Strum (one), Rest (two), Rest (three)," and then you're off to the next measure.

So why is the "whole note" symbol not referred to as a "whole 'beat'" since the symbol sends a message about beats and timing? It's called a note because it *also* acts as a note by representing a specific musical tone on the staff *as well as* relaying information about the duration of that note in a particular measure. The whole note plays a dual role, one that indicates tonality and one that indicates time value. This dual role applies to *all of the notes* in a piece of music. Each note has its special place on the staff that indicates the proper musical tone to be played on the frets of a guitar, the keys of a piano, the strings on a harp, or the keys of a wind instrument, and that same note indicates the duration of that tone. Let's now consider these other notes and their respective time values.

Once again, the whole note.

This is the half note. It's a whole note with a stem. It's played for *half* the duration of the whole note.

Here, the quarter note. It has the stem and the note head is colored in. It's played for *one quarter* the duration of the whole note.

This represents the eighth note. Again, it has the stem, the note head is colored in, and it has a flag. It is played for *one eighth* the duration of the whole note.

There are sixteenth notes, thirty-second notes, even sixty-fourth notes. These are depicted by adding additional flags to the stem. A 16th note has two flags, a 32nd note has three flags, and a 64th note has four flags.

This chart shows the relationship between different notes and their time values. It's merely another way of illustrating what I've explained in introducing the time value of notes above. Instead of saying that a half note is played for "half the duration of a whole note," this chart shows that the "timing length" of two half notes constitute the "timing length" of a whole note. The basic logic of fractions applies throughout the chart whereby two quarter notes constitute a half note, and two eighth notes constitute a quarter note.

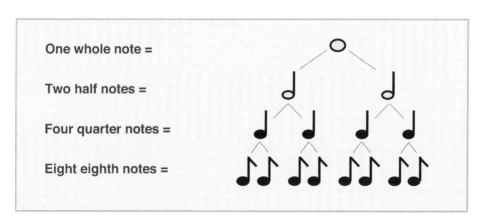

One whole note =

Two half notes =

Four quarter notes =

Eight eighth notes =

• **Reading Charts versus Reading the Staff**: The song and exercise charts that I've presented in the *Manual* are patterned after the charts that many non-reading musicians use at gigs and in the studio. These charts are usually a series of slashes that represent the beats with lines between the individual measures. When I began reading charts in live and studio settings in the 1970s, we called such charts "Nashville Shorthand" or simply, "Charts." Although I've not always included the lines to differentiate between measures in our charts, when we began to study the nuts and bolts of timing and tempo, I began using these "double-shaded" chart formats to indicate the distinction between measures:

Traditional notation is set up in a similar format. I'm presenting a typical piece of music to illustrate this similarity. In the piece below I've emphasized the **bar lines** with vertical rectangles so you can readily reference these bar lines that tell you where one measure (or bar) ends and another measure begins:

The purpose of this long-winded narrative has been to explain the nature of time signature fractions. Once again, the top number of the fraction (the numerator) tells us how many beats there are in each measure of a musical piece, and the bottom number (the denominator) tells us the beat value of those individual notes. This, of course, is the definition we started with, but I hope that the explanations I've provided help you better understand the nature of the time-signature fraction. Rest assured that I've hardly scratched the surface of "musical time" so if you're interested in additional information, there's an excellent selection of tutorials on the Internet. Please consider checking out some of these online lessons using search words like Time Signatures, Whole Notes, Half Notes, Quarter Notes, and Musical

Notation. Some sites are better than others, so snoop around and try to find one that reinforces and expands on the subjects we've addressed above.

• **Regarding Tempo**: As mentioned earlier, **tempo** is the rate of speed or the pace of a musical piece. **Time** depicts the *structure* of the beat while **Tempo** depicts the *speed* of the beat. Most sheet music has a description of the tempo immediately above the time signature at the beginning of the piece. You'll see a variety of words and phrases used to describe the speed of the music: moderately slow, swing shuffle, moderately with a beat, twist tempo, bright rock, medium bounce, steady rock, freely with motion, solid 4 beat, moderate funk, relaxed reggae, medium rock beat, slowly, with a steady beat, moderate Latin rock beat . . . You get the idea! In the world of classical music, the original Italian terminology is common with terms like *adagio*, a rate that is "quite" slow; *andante* which connotes a "walking pace;" *allegro* is a "fast and cheerful" pace; *vivace*, is a "lively" pace; or *presto* is a "very fast" pace. These are all very subjective indicators. In the early 1800s, however, a clever German inventor patented the metronome, a handy little gizmo that produces steady metrical ticks, clicks, or in today's world, beeps. Here's the standard model that you've seen perched on pianos in living rooms across the country. Newer "digital-age" metronomes are battery powered and housed in smaller casings, some smaller than a cell phone. All metronomes register beats in the same way. They all count in "**beats per minute**" (bpm) and typically produce a beat range from 40 bpm to 200 bpm. To give you an idea about how these various beats apply to practical music situations, I've listed some popular songs and their approximate beats per minute.

T-Bone Walker's "Stormy Monday"	60 beats per minute
"Amazing Grace"	80 beats per minute
"The Star-Spangled Banner"	84 beats per minute
"Happy Birthday to You"	92 beats per minute
"All My Exes Live in Texas" (G. Strait)	125 beats per minute
"Born to Run" (Bruce Springsteen)	144 beats per minute

There are a number of Internet sites that feature metronomes; there are metronome applications for cell phones; and the small portable variety are available and reasonably priced at local music stores. Metronomes are invaluable in teaching you how to set and maintain a solid groove, which in turn, is a complete necessity in playing in groups and working in recording situations. Finally, being able to refer to "beats per minute" will be helpful in working on various exercises that will be presented later in the *Manual*.

This completes the Chord & Progression section of the Manual.
We will now move on to the Matrix Method.

CHAPTER THREE
The Matrix Method

Songwriting & The DNA of Western Music

Sound & Sound Waves and Their Relationship to Music

The DNA of Western Music and Five Essential Axioms

Axiom I

Axiom II

Axiom III

Creating Chords - Major Triads

Axiom IV

The Structure of Progressions

Axiom V

Summation of Key Points

Five Axioms Revisited

Twelve Major-Key Scales

The Mechanics of Building New & Necessary Chords

Transposition Chart

THE MATRIX METHOD

The *Matrix Method* is designed to demystify music theory and make it logical, comfortable, and readily available to students at all levels. Whether you harbor long-term musical aspirations or simply play for your own enjoyment, the *Matrix Method* will be a helpful companion. Although there is no substitute for the study of standard notation and theory, I believe there are alternative avenues that can help in the development of a theoretical foundation for playing the guitar. Over the years, I have met and worked with a number of exceptional musicians who are not particularly adept at "sight reading" but who excel as studio players, performers and songwriters. Given that experience, I hold out hope for non-readers like myself and other working musicians who never invested the necessary time and effort to master the delicacies of formal musical training. If the primary mission of this *Manual* is to teach you how to play the music you want to play (which of course it is), then you will be well served by taking a good look at the *Matrix Method*.

I don't know about you, but even this short passage by Chopin scares me to death! I cannot imagine translating it into a coherent piece of music! I have the utmost respect the players who have mastered the art of reading such intricate tablature and fully

recognize that their skills are light years beyond mine. Assimilating the fine points of sight-reading is a multi-year challenge, a challenge that regretfully, I never took on. Consequently, I offer the *Matrix Method* as a helpful substitute. It is my hope that this

approach will equip you with a practical foundation and a set of tools that will help you in playing your instrument, making recordings, working in a studio, and in "speaking music" with other musicians, engineers, and producers.

In previous lessons and exercises, we have touched on a number of the concepts that appear in the forthcoming analysis. We have considered notes, whole steps, half steps, chords, progressions and an array of other components that are essential to performance guitar. The following essay ties together these assorted elements into a coherent theory through a series of common rules that I call Axioms that apply to the overall instructional mission of the *Manual*.

The essay is a segment from an academic piece written several years ago about songwriting and the live-music scene in Austin, Texas during the 1970s. The segment is titled, "Songwriting and the DNA of Western Music" and the larger piece is titled, "The Austin Music Scene in the 1970s - Songs & Songwriters." I was deeply entrenched in the Austin scene of that period and I used it as a cultural setting to explore some of the common elements of the *Matrix Method*. For the most part, I am reproducing the essay as it was originally written. There are certain parts of the essay that address technical aspects of musicology that might prove a bit cumbersome, but I've provided text box inserts like the one to the right to help clarify such information. These text boxes play another role. If there is a subject addressed in a particular box that you are not interested in, simply pass over that box and continue with the essay. Similarly, the footnotes, although informative, are optional.

> Text Boxes will supplement the information presented in the main text.

There are parts of the essay that wander from the basic theme of guitar instruction. I deal with subjects like songwriting, playing in a band, working as a sideman in support of singer-songwriters and even delve into some aspects of simple electronics as they apply to notes and frequencies. I hope that these various "wanderings" will prove beneficial to your overall understanding of the guitar, how it is played, and how you can incorporate this unique instrument into your lifestyle and your personal musical mission. With this in mind, I have provided a summation of the key points presented in the essay at the end of the *Matrix Method* essay. This summation will provide the various Axioms and related rules as well as certain charts that will serve as convenient reference tools.

Songwriting and the DNA of Western Music

The act of writing a song is a complex undertaking that involves an inexhaustible set of variables. The lyrical effort depends on the writer's level of literary competency, experience, or motivation. It might depend on their philosophical or spiritual disposition, their emotional state, or their grasp of the relevant material. Their writing effort might depend on a professional songwriting obligation or a grand artistic goal. The variables associated with creating the lyrical content of a song—the story, the plot, the message, the mood, or the moral—are as vast as the writer's imagination and the circumstances surrounding the writing process. The musical aspects of a song however—the notes, the chords, the key, and the related musical components—are fundamentally more manageable. There are musical methodologies that have developed over the centuries that largely define how music is written, performed and passed from generation to generation. Music theory is a greybeard among intellectual pursuits and is steeped in empiricism and repetitive practice. The challenge of musical composition in all its complicated configurations essentially boils down to twelve basic building blocks—a dozen seminal components of musical DNA. The entirety of Western music is built upon only twelve distinct notes.

I arrive at this hypothesis through practical experience. As mentioned, I am not trained in traditional music theory, I cannot read music, and I have had very few formal music lessons. My musical training is a product of playing by ear, learning songs by listening to records, by watching other musicians, and by teaching entry-level guitar students since 1966. As a young guitar teacher, I was able to piece together some simple mathematical relationships between the notes on the fretboard, chord structures and progressions. These observations evolved into a system that I retrospectively call a "matrix method" of guitar instruction. The matrix format is based on the six strings of a standard guitar and the first twelve frets on the neck that facilitate a complete octave—six strings and twelve individual notes on the fretboard that yield an elongated 6x12 matrix. I did not study scales as a beginning player, but by studying the sequence of notes up the neck on a string-by-string basis, I was able to ascertain where the whole-step and half-step intervals fell and how they related from one string to the next.

The guitar is a very logical instrument. If for example, you play an E chord in the first position (which is located at the end of the neck next to the tuning pegs), you can slide that fingering position up one fret, "barre" the open strings with your first finger on the first fret and instantly create an F chord. If you slide this configuration up another two frets, you have a G chord. To make the same transition on a piano you would have to learn the specific fingering positions for the E chord, then learn the F chord, and finally the G chord. You cannot simply "slide" the same fingering position up to a higher register on the piano to produce a different chord. The essential structure of the guitar allows the player to create new chords by simply moving up and down the neck. Although the guitar is initially much more physically demanding—for beginners it is actually painful to apply the pressure necessary to make the notes sound clearly—it is much more accessible from a structural point of view. As a teacher of beginning guitar, I was intrigued with the uniform matrix methodology in forming new chords. I found that the logic of creating new chords, particularly the techniques associated with barre chords, was simple and motivational to beginning players. Despite the physical challenge of reaching for these new chords up and down the neck, aspiring students readily understood the mathematical relationships between the sequence of notes and chords. They "got it" and from a teacher's perspective, that was encouraging.

> What I'm touching on here is the essence of the barre chord technique I have mentioned throughout the *Manual*. This is a small taste of what is to come in the next section which addresses barre chords. Learning how to play and use these formations is truly an enlightening experience because so much of what you have been learning begins to fall into place through practical and logical application.

I began applying the mechanics of this guitar matrix to the connections between notes, chords and chord progressions and developed a set of Axioms that relate to the process of making music on the guitar. These Axioms are practical learning tools that provide an alternative to the cumbersome and extensive task of studying traditional music theory. I have presented these fundamental propositions to beginning guitar students to equip them with a pragmatic foundation in theory that they can readily incorporate into their day-to-day playing. By utilizing these basic rules the aspiring guitarist can easily create basic chord progressions, form minor or seventh chords, transpose from one key to another, determine which relative minor fits with which progression, and access other tricks of the trade that sound far more difficult than they are. It is an accessible approach that generates immediate gratification and a sense of accomplishment. These Axioms enable players at all levels to communicate with their fellow musicians, a skill that is essential in live performance, band, and recording situations.

A shared language or, more accurately, a jargon, is essential in the learning process, the songwriting process, and in all other aspects of contemporary guitar playing. A common jargon is essential in establishing a "**cognitive link**" between what we *hear* and what we *call* it, especially when discussing genres, sub-genres and musical styles. Developing such a "**cognitive link**" between sound and language helps to alleviate the common practice of lining up a litany of modifiers to describe a style, a genre, or a musical texture. As an example, consider the following fictional description of a young artist's recent CD release: "Her music is a cross between blues, rock, jazz, and country and represents a fresh approach to pop music." This reads like hundreds of music reviews but tells us very little about the fabric and feel of the music in question. In an attempt to avoid this rambling and ineffective technique, I am offering this simple matrix method to establish a common vocabulary to better understand the structure and characteristics of the popular compositions under study. The narrative beginning in the forthcoming pages offers several simple Axioms that map out the structural relationships between notes, chords and progressions relative to the contemporary songs and sounds of the seventies, and by extension, to popular music styles in the decades that followed.

In talking about this so-called "**cognitive link**," I am expressing my concerns about how journalists, historians and teachers often write about popular music. My sentiments can be expressed by offering this austere observation: "My 'blues' aren't necessarily your 'blues.'" To one observer the "blues" might mean the music of the early 20th-century renowned guitarist Robert Johnson and his highly complex finger-picking style on the acoustic guitar. To another observer, the "blues" might mean the high-energy licks of the mid-20th-century electric guitar stylist Muddy Waters. And to a third observer, the "blues" might mean the rock-flavored versions of classic blues styles as performed and popularized by musicians who were largely linked to the "British Invasion" of the later 60s and early 70s. Are all of these styles "blues?" Well, yes. They share common musical threads, but they sound noticeably different, and each style offers a specific niche in the ongoing development of American popular music. The same observation could be made about jazz, folk, rock, country and many other popular genres and styles. Consequently, it is important to establish a common vocabulary so that when we are *talking* about acoustic Delta Blues (which of course suggests Robert Johnson), we are all *hearing* a similar tape from our mental musical memory banks. In other words, we are "establishing a '**cognitive link**' between what we *hear* and what we *call* it." In a similar fashion, the teacher and the student must speak the same language and apply it to the same sounds just as the members of a band must embrace the same musical jargon to create the same sounds they are trying to express in their studio recordings and their live performances.

As mentioned, there are twelve basic notes in Western music. Music in Asia, Africa or in other parts of the world might incorporate more and/or different notes, but in Western music—the musical styles that developed in Europe during the Middle Ages that immigrated to the New World beginning in the 16th century—there are only twelve basic notes. A note, according to *The Concise Oxford Dictionary of Music* is a single sound of a given musical pitch and duration, also called a tone in America. More specifically, a note coincides with a particular frequency. The "A" note just above middle C on a piano oscillates at 440 cycles per second (440 Hz). This is a worthy example because A440 is the note accepted by International Organization for Standardization as the general tuning standard for musical pitch. And like A440, all musical notes sound at distinctive frequencies within the spectrum of human hearing that ranges from 20 cycles per second (20 Hz) to roughly 20,000 cycles per second (20,000 Hz).

Sound & Sound Waves and Their Relationship to Music

So what is all this gibberish about frequencies, oscillations, cycles per second and symbols like Hz? To understand these terms, it helps to know a little bit about *sound*. At its most basic level, sound is a mechanical wave that is transmitted through a physical medium (usually air) that we can hear. A sound wave disrupts the air causing a microscopic pressure field that our brains interpret as a sound when that wave hits our eardrums and makes them vibrate. A typical sound wave, as drawn by scientists, appears in the diagram to the right. A sound wave is essentially an invisible thread of energized air molecules that moves back and forth at a steady rate. The faster the thread vibrates, the higher the frequency and the higher the pitch. The slower the thread vibrates, the lower 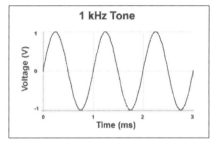 frequency and the lower the pitch. To visualize this concept of vibration, strike the lower E string on your guitar, watch it carefully, and you will see the rapid, vibrating motion of the string. It is this vibration, enhanced by the acoustic properties of the guitar, that creates the microscopic pressure field that creates a sound wave. It is this pressure field or "wave" that travels through the air on its way to the listener. The individual molecules do not move through the air, they simply facilitate the movement of the wave. As individual molecules vibrate, they energize their neighboring molecules to create a rippling effect that advances the wave to the listener. By exploring the physical properties of sound waves, we can address and understand these technical terms and significantly expand our grasp of practical audio theory and guitar playing.

The following illustration shows the connection between the physical properties of the vibrating molecules that move sound from the source to the listener and the graphic representation of the sound wave. It shows how the molecules group together in clusters to create pulses of strong sound pressure followed by pulses of weak sound pressure and how the graphic configuration of a sound wave reflects these peaks or "crests" and valleys or "troughs." The term sound pressure relates to the degree of force that the vibrating molecules exert on the eardrum. When molecular clusters hit the eardrum, they cause it to vibrate which our brain then interprets as sound. A tightly packed pulse (represented by the wave crest) puts more pressure on the eardrum than a loosely packed pulse (represented by the wave trough). The greater the pressure, the greater the vibration of the eardrum, and the greater the sound perceived by our audio senses. Volume therefore, is a function of sound pressure and is commonly measured in "decibels." A decibel (dB) is a mathematical formula that measures the *intensity* of sound waves that hit the eardrum. The graphic representation of the sound wave below is the shape of the wave or the *waveform*.

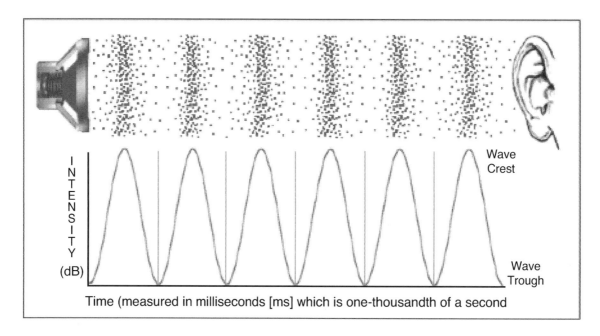

Let us address the technical terms associated with the sound wave by analyzing a statement I made earlier in the essay: "The 'A' note just above middle C on a piano oscillates at 440 cycles per second (440 Hz)." To "oscillate at 440 cycles per second" means that the sound wave goes up and down or "cycles" from its crest to its trough and back again 440 times in a given second. This rate of movement is commonly known as "frequency." In simple terms, frequency tells us how *frequently* a sound wave moves up and down or oscillates in a second. This phenomenon is measured in "hertz," abbreviated Hz. The technical standard for hertz defines one hertz as a unit of frequency that equals one cycle per second. That is, the sound wave moves through a complete cycle from its trough to its crest then back to its trough over the duration of a second. For a visual perspective of cycles per second or frequencies, consider the sound wave above. It represents a frequency of 1 kHz or "one kilohertz." The "k" in the designation is a multiplier of 1,000 so 1 kHz means one thousand hertz. The vertical axis represents the strength or intensity of the sound wave which is measured in decibels. The horizontal Time Line is measured in milliseconds. This suggests that the sound wave above, if charted out for an entire second, would require many pages to graph its considerable length. Remember however, that we're talking about molecular-sized sound waves and that these drawings are only two-dimensional representations of a three-dimensional event in nature.

I mentioned earlier that the frequencies audible to humans range from 20 Hz to 20,000 Hz. The frequency range of the human voice runs from approximately 300 Hz to 3,400 Hz. To get a feel for how these various frequencies apply to what you actually hear and how they apply to your efforts to play, sing, and make music, we need to present a few more brief examples. To no small degree, audio engineering focuses on the manipulation of sound waves, so a couple of real-world examples will be helpful. The purpose of the following examples is to identify sounds you have probably heard in your day-to-day activities and link those sound to visual representations of sound waves. Again, we are trying to establish a 'cognitive link' between what we *hear* and what we *call* it.

1. In light of what we have explored so far about frequencies, I am hoping that you can make some sense of the following statement: "mains hum" or "power-line hum" is an audible oscillation of alternating current at the frequency of the mains electrical source, which is usually 50 Hz or 60 Hz, depending on the local power line frequency. If you have spent much time around musicians, bands, or sound equipment, you have probably heard the term, "sixty-cycle hum." That is what this sentence is describing. When we plug our amplifiers or sound systems into wall sockets to tap the necessary AC ("alternating current" or more commonly, "electricity") to power up our equipment, that power source often comes with some extra electromagnetic baggage. That extra baggage is a low, 60-cycle hum that is picked up and  broadcast through the instrument amplifiers and the P.A. system. You can remedy this situation by either switching the ground on the various amplifiers which adjusts the flow of electricity, use another power source, or move your amp to avoid the electromagnet field responsible for the hum. A 60-cycle waveform, or 60 Hz, would look roughly like the illustration above.

    2. The waveform represented in Parts I and II above has a frequency of 1 kHz or 1,000 Hz. That frequency, reproduced just below, yields a B note that is two octaves above the middle B note on a piano. The corresponding note on the guitar would be the B note on the high E string played at the 7th fret. In other words, that B note represented above, sounds at 1,000 cycles per second or 1 kHz.

    3. Imagine going to hear a live band in a small club. As they get ready to kick off their set, they are checking their microphones by chanting the proverbial "Testing One, Two, Three." As the sound technician works through the final adjustments, you suddenly hear a biting, high-frequency squeal that sends you diving under the table! That's feedback! Feedback is caused by an audio signal, a voice for example, that travels through the microphones, out through the P.A. speakers, then back through the microphone to create what's called a "feedback loop." Although feedback loops can happen at any audible frequency, "high-end" feedback is by far the most caustic and is usually a product of frequencies in "the thousands." A typical screech of this sort is in the 3,000- to 5,000-cycle range (3 kHz to 5 kHz) and produces a sound wave that looks like the illustration just above.

    4. As the frequencies get higher, the waveforms become more compact and dense. The depiction just below illustrates high-end sound waves that probably register in the 12 kHz to 18 kHz range. Obviously packing in 12,000 to 18,000 cycles into a time-sensitive sequence makes for cramped quarters! Although these graphic representations are not scientifically accurate, they should be helpful in making a connection between the technical definitions of sound waves, how they are graphically represented, and ultimately, how they sound.

To sum up this Sound and Sound Waves adventure, we will list and review some of the terms and definitions we have considered in the sections above:

• **Frequency**: The rate at which a vibration occurs that constitutes a wave, either in a physical medium (sound waves usually through the air for example), or in an electromagnetic field (as in radio waves and light), that is generally measured in one-second intervals. A frequency boils down to how many cycles or wavelengths pass by a given point over the course of a second.

• **Oscillate**: To move back and forth at a regular speed. Sound waves *oscillate* to produce sound.

• **Hertz** (Hz): A unit of frequency equal to one cycle per second.

• **Cycle**: One complete performance of a vibration or electric oscillation. The wave cycle is the journey a sound wave makes from its trough to its crest and back to the trough again. Or, if you'd rather, it is the trip the sound wave makes from its crest to its trough and back to the crest. This complete cycle is known as the *wavelength*.

• **Wavelength**: As mentioned above, it is the complete wave cycle from trough to trough or from crest to crest.

• **Waveform**: The shape and form of a sound wave that is moving through a physical medium. The waveform generally refers to the graphic representation of the sound wave.

• **Wave Crest**: The point in the wave cycle that exhibits the maximum amount of molecular oscillation. Accordingly, it is the point in the wave cycle that has the most energy.

• **Wave Trough**: The point in the wave cycle that exhibits the minimum amount of molecular oscillation. Accordingly, it is the point in the wave cycle that has the least energy.

• **Decibel**: A unit used to measure the intensity of a sound or the power of an electronic signal by comparing it to a specific or implied reference level. In common usage, decibel means loudness.

• **Kilohertz**: A measure of frequency equivalent to 1,000 (one thousand) cycles per second.

• **Megahertz**: A measure of frequency equivalent to 1,000,000 (one million) cycles per second.

• **Gigahertz**: A measure of frequency equivalent to 1,000,000,000 (one billion) cycles per second.

Before moving on to the next section, I would like to comment on several interchangeable terms, specifically, **half step** and **semitone** and **whole step** and **whole tone**. As previously discussed, to move up or down the fretboard by a single fret is to move a half step. This single-fret interval between two notes or tones is also known as a semitone. To move up or down the fretboard by two frets is to move a whole step. This double-fret interval between two notes is also known as a whole tone. The interval between an E note on the guitar (playing the open 6th string for example) and an F note (6th string, 1st fret) is a half step and/or a semitone. The interval between an F note on the guitar (playing the 6th string at the 1st fret) and a G note (playing the 6th string at the 3rd fret) is a whole-step or a whole tone.

There is much more to consider about this business of Sound, Frequencies and Sound Waves, but what we have covered so far should be adequate to illustrate how frequencies determine the hierarchy of notes and, at a more fundamental level, how energy translates into sound. We'll now move into an essential phase of the Matrix Method that analyzes how these notes and sounds fit together into a logical structure and how that structure informs our ability to understand and play the music we love. We'll review our basic inventory of notes, then we'll consider how to create scales, how to blend notes into chords, how to shape these chords into progressions and the songs we want to play. To make sense of all of this, we'll study the simple mathematical associations between these various notes, scales, chords and progressions by considering and applying five Axioms or "truths" that establish the rules of the road in creating and playing popular music. To begin this phrase, we'll return to those twelve basic notes that represent the harmonic DNA of Western music.

THE DNA OF WESTERN MUSIC
and
FIVE ESSENTIAL AXIOMS

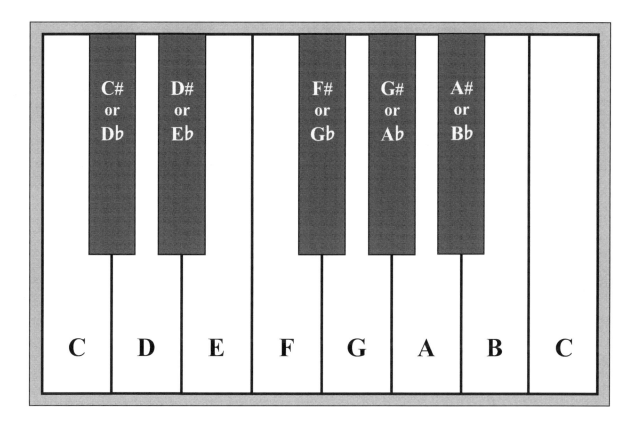

This piano section illustrates the 12 basic tones upon which all Western music is based. Please note that these twelve notes represent one complete octave and that the piano's keyboard is simply a series of these octaves from the lower register to the higher notes. For our purposes, it might be convenient to present this "twelve-pack" in a linear fashion or as a Periodic Table of Notes:

These observations suggest the first Axiom that applies to the Matrix Method and to the foundations of making popular music:

Axiom I: **There are twelve notes used in Western music. These twelve unique tones are the basic building blocks or essential DNA components from which all composition and theory follows.**

The sequence of notes beginning at middle C and continuing up the scale through the B note that precedes the C octave note comprise the "Periodic Table of Notes." These same twelve notes repeat every new octave whether ascending or descending the piano keyboard. Further, each new octave voicing of a note *ascending* the scale sounds at *twice* the frequency of its lower predecessor. Middle C for example sounds at 262 Hz and the octave C sounds at 524 Hz. Each new octave voicing of a note *descending* the scale

> Here, your knowledge of frequencies comes into play.

sounds at *half* the frequency of its higher predecessor. The same middle C that sounds at 262 Hz sounds at 131 Hz in the lower octave. The black keys on the piano signify the sharps (#) and flats (*b*). The black key immediately following the middle C in the keyboard illustration above labeled C# or D*b* actually depicts a single note. There is no difference in the tone or frequency of a C# or a D*b*, it is simply two names for the same

note and calling that note a C# or a D*b* is based on the context in which it is used. This holds true for all black keys on the keyboard and by extension, to all "sharp and flat" notes in all musical settings. Further, the tonal relationships on the piano apply to all musical instruments and all musical relationships.

> In traditional musical notation there are instances where it's important to distinguish between a C# and a D*b* for example, or between a D# and an E*b*, an F# and a G*b*, a G# and an A*b*, or an A# and a B*b* but this relates to minor scales and other configurations that are beyond the scope of this study. The bottom line is this: These conjoining sharp and flat notes are the same *frequency* that produces the same *tone*.

Also worth mentioning is the concept of intervals, what we have been calling half steps and whole steps. The black keys on the piano are placed irregularly between the white keys. This arrangement reflects the standard sequence of the basic twelve notes. The intervals of some notes are whole steps while the intervals between other notes are half steps. The interval between C and D for example is a whole step, while the interval

C and the adjacent black key, C#/Db, is a half step, and the interval between that same C#/Db note and the adjacent D is a half step. Following the notes *chromatically* up the scale therefore is a sequence of half steps.[6] This illustrates an essential characteristic of the Periodic Table of notes. There is a half step between E and F and between B and C. There are no passing notes between these notes and this applies in all circumstances. The significance of this simple observation comes into sharper focus in the process of building scales which is addressed below. These observations regarding the static relationship between E and F and between B and C suggest the second Axiom:

> **Axiom II: There is always a half step between E and F and between B and C. (In terms of the Periodic Table of Notes therefore, there are no E#/Fb or B#/Cb notes.)**[7]

These two Axioms define the twelve basic building blocks, their sequence, and their structural relationships. These Axioms also illustrate several basic mathematical observations regarding the foundation and creation of musical scales. Every note provides the basic tone for its signature scale. Accordingly, there are C, D, E, F, G, A, and B scales as well as C#/Db, D#/Eb, F#/Gb, and G#/Ab scales that accommodate the sharp and flat keys. All of these scales have three things in common that relate to the matrix method and the Axioms offered herein.[8] The first two commonalities have been mentioned: All scales are derivatives of twelve basic notes (Axiom I) and all scales reflect that there is always a half step between E and F and between B and C (Axiom II). The third commonality has to do with how scales are structurally sequenced, which provides the groundwork for the third Axiom:

---

[6] "Chromatically" in this context means moving from one note to the next adjoining note. Technically, a chromatic scale is a musical scale with twelve distinct pitches each a semitone apart. In other words, a chromatic scale is twelve sequential notes (the basic twelve building blocks) linked by half steps or semitones.

[7] Several of my more enlightened colleagues with backgrounds in traditional music theory tell me that in certain circumstances the notes E#, Fb or B#, Cb are notated as such. Nonetheless, there is no specific frequency assigned to these notes and the notation of an E# or an Fb would yield the same tonal frequency as an E or an F just as the notation of a B# or Cb would yield the same tonal frequency of a B or a C. This observation is in keeping with footnote 7 above.

[8] Scales have many things in common, but as mentioned, the three commonalities suggested above relate to the simplified matrix method and purposefully avoids a probing (and probably a far more accurate) analysis of scales.

Axiom III: In any given eight-note *major* scale, there is always a half step between the *third* and the *fourth* note of the sequence and between the *seventh* and *eighth* note of the sequence. All other intervals are whole steps.[9]

To illustrate this axiom and to see how it interconnects with the initial two axioms, we will explore the structure of a C scale. To that end, we will lay out a complete chromatic octave in C that will serve as an inventory of notes. By the term "chromatic octave in C," I am referring to each note between a C note and the octave of that C note. This would include twelve distinct notes—our "Periodic Table of Notes"—as well as a 13th note, the octave of the initial C. From these notes, we will map out a C scale by incorporating the directives in Axiom I and Axiom II.

This inventory shows the natural half steps between E and F and between B and C as mentioned in Axiom II.

To continue with the C scale, we will "superimpose" the directives mentioned in Axiom III on our thirteen-note inventory and select the notes we need for that scale. We will begin with the lower C note, then advance a whole step to D, advance another whole step to D, and advance another whole step to E. Because we have arrived at the interval between the third and fourth note, we will move only a half step to F. We will continue with a whole step to G, a whole step to A, and a whole step to B. Our final move, the interval between the seventh and the eighth note, requires a half step which brings us back to another C note that is the octave of our original C note. The numbers, 1 through 8, below the notes in the darker boxes, represent the notes necessary for the scale.

---

[9] From a technical point of view, Axiom III applies only to major scales. For that reason, I included the word "major" into the sentence above and italicized it. For the purposes of the *Matrix Method* however, Axiom III has merit: The mission at hand is to facilitate a dialogue between non-music-reading players. In this effort, I believe the *Matrix Method* is helpful.

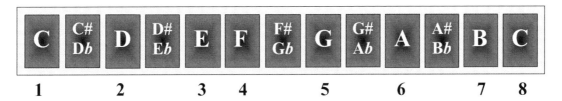

1   2   3   4   5   6   7   8

This selection process yields the following C scale:

1   2   3   4   5   6   7   8

The selection process also illustrates the confluence of Axioms I, II, and III:

1. We began by laying out our Periodical Table of Notes beginning with a C. We chose a C because we were interested in creating a C scale. We could just as easily have begun with a D or an A#/B*b* for that matter (Axiom I).

2. We laid out our note inventory with the appropriate half steps between E & F and B & C (Axiom II).

3. We applied the appropriate "intervals" that were mentioned in Axiom III by observing whole steps between notes 1 & 2, notes 2 & 3, notes 4 & 5, notes 5 & 6, notes 6 & 7, and half steps between notes 3 & 4 and 7 & 8 (Axiom III).

Before moving on to a final example of building a scale by using our three Axioms, I'd like to comment on the unique nature of the C scale. The C scale is the only major scale that has no sharps or flats. The confluence of our three Axioms produces this singular scale, a scale that some call a natural or perfect scale. The scale's simplicity makes it a very popular scale (as well as a popular Key) for beginning students.

As a final example of the practical utility of Axioms I, II and III, we will build a D scale. Once again, we will lay out the basic notes from the Periodic Table of Notes beginning with a D note and ending with the octave of that D. And, once again, we will incorporate the directives from Axiom III to select the appropriate notes for our scale. This selection process is illustrated by the following chart in which the darker boxes represent the chosen notes:

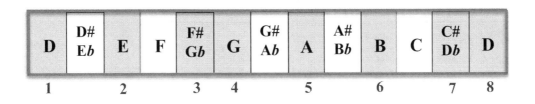

1   2   3   4   5   6   7   8

This selection process yields the following D scale:

D	E	F# Gb	G	A	B	C# Db	D
1	2	3	4	5	6	7	8

By incorporating the directives of Axioms I, II, and III, you can create a scale in any given key by first laying out your Periodic Table of Notes beginning with the "key note," by remembering that there is always a half step between E and F and between B and C, and finally by remembering that there is always a half-step between the third and the fourth note and between the seventh and the eighth note. I've presented a set of scales that covers each individual key at the end of this chapter. See: "THE TWELVE MAJOR KEY SCALES" on page 97.

As we will see in the pages that follow, these three Axioms coupled with two additional Axioms, enable the students to create chords, which are defined as a combination of three or more tones that sound together in harmony, and chart out progressions, which are collections of chords common to a particular key. Progressions form the harmonic foundation of popular songs. There are countless well-known songs in the American canon that contain only three chords like "Home on the Range," "Clementine," or "Battle Hymn of the Republic." Most classic blues songs have only three basic chords; pop songs like "Rock Around the Clock," "Hound Dog," even "Louie Louie" are all three-chord wonders; folk music and country songs generally embody a three- to four-chord format and even the National Anthem in a simple arrangement has only five chords. The grand majority of hit songs over the last 150 years are based on fundamental chords and basic chord progressions.

Creating Chords - Major Triads

Forming a chord involves combining three notes of a particular scale, the first note, the third note and the fifth note. This combination of three notes is commonly

C	D	E	F	G	A	B	C
1	2	3	4	5	6	7	8

called a triad. A simple C chord therefore includes the base C note, the third note of the scale, E, and the fifth note of the scale, G. In other words, it is a "1-3-5 triad." This particular triad is a major triad because it creates a major chord. The major triad is the basis for other types of chords as we'll see below. The major triad is also the subject of the next Axiom:

> **Axiom IV**: **To assemble the basic building blocks of a major chord in any particular key, you combine the first, the third, and the fifth notes of that scale in that designated key. This is called a Major Triad.**

Forming other chords beyond the major triad is largely a matter of modifying the basic triad. A Cm (C-minor) chord for example, is rooted in the major triad except one of the notes is modified. The third note is flatted by dropping it a half step (E to E*b*) to yield a Cm triad: C,

I will provide an overview of the techniques involved in creating new chords by modifying the major triad at the end of this section.

E*b* and G. A C7 (C-seventh) chord begins with the basic triad and adds a fourth note which is the flatted seventh note of the scale—B is the seventh note of a C scale and is flatted by taking the note down a half step to produce a B*b*—which yields the following C7 combination: C, E, G + B*b*. All chords are similarly designed, each with their unique structural formula. To create an augmented chord you add this, to form a major-seventh chord, you lower that, or to create a suspended-fourth chord you tinker with the basic scale by employing a different chord formula. This fourth Axiom enables an aspiring student to map out challenging new chords and expand their musical vocabulary. To introduce the fifth and final Axiom, we need to revisit the structure of progressions.

The Structure of Progressions
(Some of this material has been addressed earlier in the Manual)

Progressions involve combining chords into familiar groupings to create the songs we have used in the *Manual* and in fact, most popular songs in Western Music. Through the centuries, specific chord combinations have become common fare because they sound pleasing and *feel* familiar to Western musical sensitivities. The most common progressions in Western music are anchored in simple three-chord structures derived from the first chord, the fourth chord, and the fifth chord associated with a particular scale. A standard C progression for example would include the major triad derived from the root note of C, followed by the major triad built from the fourth note of the scale, F, and completed with the major triad derived from the fifth note of the scale, G. In traditional music jargon the first chord is known as the "tonic," the fourth chord is the "subdominant" and the fifth chord is called the "dominant." In modern parlance, the tonic is generally called the one-chord, the subdominant is the four-chord, and the dominant is called the five-chord. These are either written as Arabic numerals, 1-4-5, or in Roman numerals, I-IV-V. Therefore, the common phrase, "1-4-5," simply refers to a standard three-chord progression. This suggests the following Axiom:

> **Axiom V: To assemble the basic building blocks of a chord progression in a particular key, reference the three major triads based on the first, the fourth, and the fifth notes of that scale. This will yield the essential three-chord sequence of the harmonic series commonly called a chord progression.**

Just as forming other chords beyond the fundamental major triad is largely a matter of modifying that triad, forming expanded progressions to include complimentary chords is largely a matter of adding other chords based on that scale onto the basic I-IV-V chordal mix. I will comment on the mechanics of expanding progressions in the summary of key points at the end of this section.

This information on progressions provides the essential tools to wade into the contemporary musical jargon that is relevant to this study of songs and songwriters. It is a form of "music-speak" that I initially learned as "Nashville shorthand" that enables popular-music practitioners to communicate regardless of their level of competency in reading music or what is technically known as "standard notation" that involves the use of classical symbols written on a staff or stave.[10] Nashville shorthand is simply a phrase that many Austin musicians adopted during the 1970s. The technique has other names. Some refer to the practice as "reading charts" others refer to it as the "Nashville Number

---

[10] The staff, or stave, is a set of five horizontal lines and four spaces that represent different musical notes of a specific pitch.

System," and there are other names and variations of this ad hoc notation. Scholar and classically trained musician Hugh Sparks makes the following observation in his 1984 dissertation, *Stylistic Development and Compositional Processes of Selected Solo Singer/songwriters in Austin, Texas*, in describing the communication techniques used by Austin musician Wink Tyler and his band: "[Tyler] could read Roman numeral harmonic progression charts though he, like the studio musicians in Nashville, used Arabic numerals [rather than Roman numerals]."[11] Sparks singles out Tyler because his band was known for their ability to accompany country music stars passing through Austin in need of a band. Tyler and company would acquire a song list from the traveling singer and chart out the material in advance by listening to their records. Or, given their level of proficiency, they could simply "wing it" by subtly communicating the "number system" on stage.

This is how various performances and jam sessions often unfolded in Austin during the 1970s. If a new songwriter came to town or was passing through and wanted to use a band or a few extra musicians, players from Austin's pool of support musicians would gather for the task. In this fashion, writers like Guy Clark, Townes Van Zandt, or Keith Sykes could readily pick up sidemen in Austin if they wanted to expand their stage show. In such an impromptu setting, it was common for one of the musicians who might be familiar with a certain song the performer was going to play to mention to the others that "this is a 1-2-4-5 in C with a 6-minor in the bridge." This meant the song was in C, the verse contained a C, D, F and G that there would be a A-minor in the bridge. The common practice was to sit back and listen to the first verse, discern the structure and layer in additional instruments as the song developed. This phenomenon was accurately described by long-time guitar and bass sideman, Travis Holland:

> Now, as to the ability of the musicians in Austin to just go from one band to another without spending weeks rehearsing, well, most of the people had several years of music experience under their belt. They were comfortable on stage, they might be familiar to a certain extent with [the songwriter's] material, and they usually knew the other pickers in the band. But mostly, they were receptive

---

[11] Sparks, Hugh Cullen. *Stylistic Development and Compositional Processes of Selected Solo Singer/Songwriters in Austin, Texas.* Presented to the Faculty of the Graduate School of The University of Texas at Austin in Partial Fulfillment of the Requirements for the Degree of Doctor of Philosophy, p. 46.

enough to listen and watch while they were playing, to figure out what was going on and what the band was trying to do. They had a willingness to lay back and figure out what was supposed to happen. And if you've got that, you can play with anybody. That was why they were flexible. It wasn't because the music was the same from one songwriter to the next. Sidemen didn't come to Austin much. Because if they did, they had better be damned good, if they wanted to earn a living there.[12]

In the situation that Holland describes, one of the players who might be familiar with the song structures would be communicating the changes through hand signals or subtle verbal cues. This was a common practice on stage and in the recording studio where such "shorthand" charts were routinely used rather than formal musical notation. One aspect of Holland's observation is worth highlighting, specifically, that the support players "were receptive enough to listen and watch while they were playing," in an effort "to figure out what was going on and what the band was trying to do." This illustrates a basic theme common to the experienced sidemen of the period—a reverence for the song. Good musicians let the song tell them what to play.

---

[12] Holland, Travis. *Texas Genesis A Wild Ride through Texas Progressive Country Music 1963 - 1978, with Digressions, as Seen through the Warped Mind of Travis Holland as told to Mike Williams.* (Austin: B. F. Deal Publishing, 1978).

Summation of Key Points Presented
in the *Matrix Method* and in the Essay:
"Songwriting and the DNA of Western Music"

The following pages are designed as a "reference source" to provide an easy-access format to review the main points I have presented in the *Matrix Method* and the essay. Let me mention once again that the *Matrix Method* is not traditional music theory. In that capacity, it falls far short. It is merely an effort to help the aspiring student to understand how notes, chords, and progressions fall together in a coherent, logical way. Also, it is designed to enable the student to "speak music" with his or her fellow players and music-making associates. If my multi-decade adventure as a professional guitar player is any indication, I can say with confidence that the *Matrix Method* works as a viable tool for sharing essential information in the rehearsal room, on stage, or in the studio. What follows are the vital terms, ideas, and directives presented in the *Matrix Method* and in the essay.

Cognitive Link: In a general sense, "cognitive" relates to the process of learning through reasoning or perception. By extension, a cognitive link is fundamentally a "learning link," and the link we are trying to establish in this study is the connection between what we *hear* and what we *call* it. For our purposes, a cognitive link is a "language link" and suggests a common jargon shared by musicians, musicologists, recording engineers, producers, and related music makers. In short, it's a tool designed to put us on the same musical page or, in the digital age, on the same "wavelength!"

Sound & Sound Waves: There is no need to reprint the terms and definitions we have consider above. The study of sound, sound waves, and all the physics that applies to these terms is a vast subject and I have barely scratched the surface. If you are interested in the physics of sound, there are a number of great websites to visit. Just search the Internet for any terms you are interested in and you will find countess tutorials that are far more sophisticated and accurate than the ad hoc definitions I have provided. Let me suggest one website that's worth a visit:

Media College. com (http://www.mediacollege.com/audio/tone/)

This site features the following link, "Download samples of audio tone." As the title suggests, the link provides a representative collection of audio tones, specifically, 100Hz, 250Hz, 440Hz, 1kHz and 10kHz. I suggest this site because it offers and excellent opportunity to establish that very important connection between what we *hear* and what we *call* it. Listening to the actual frequencies is very helpful in making that cognitive link and understanding the tones you are producing on your guitar.

The Five Axioms and the DNA of Western Music

Axiom I: There are twelve notes used in Western music. These twelve unique tones are the basic building blocks or essential DNA components from which all composition and theory follows.

The Twelve Seminal Notes

Axiom II: There is always a half step between E and F and between B and C. (In terms of the Periodic Table of Tones therefore, there are no E#/F*b* or B#/C*b* notes).

A good way to keep this idea fresh is to refer to the E strings on your guitar. As you know, the 1st and the 6th strings produce the same sequence of notes in different octaves, and by simply playing and identifying the notes up and down the neck, you can easily see where these half steps fall: They fall between the open string, E, and the next note, F, at the first fret, and between the B note on the 7th fret and the next note, C, on the 8th fret.

Axiom III: In any given eight-note *major* scale, there is always a half step between the third and the fourth note of the sequence and between the seventh and eighth note of the sequence. All other intervals are whole steps.

When you are thinking about **scales**, whether you' are building, interpreting, or practicing them, keep in mind these two key number sets, **3&4** and **7&8**. This is where the designated half steps fall. I realize that I am repeating what's presented in Axiom III, but I wanted to drive home the point that the key numbers regarding **scales** are 3&4 and 7&8. Do not confuse these numbers with the numbers that relate to creating **chords**. Those numbers, **1+3+5**, designate the essential building blocks of the **major triad** as explained in Axiom IV below. Also, do not confuse your "scale" numbers with the number set that relates to basic **progressions**, specifically, **1,4**, and **5** that signify the three basic chords of a progression as explained in Axiom V.

As I mentioned previously, I am providing a chart of all the various major scales on the next page. It would be great if you could memorize these various scales, but more importantly, you need to understand the mechanics of building these scales. This of course brings us full circle to the "Twelve Seminal Notes." To create a major scale, you take the appropriate notes from the 12-note inventory and lay them out in whole-step intervals with the exception of the third and fourth notes and the seventh and eighth notes which require a half-step interval.

THE TWELVE MAJOR KEY SCALES

Notice the shaded positions: These are shaded to remind the reader that in forming major scales there is always a half-step between interval 3 & 4 and 7 & 8.

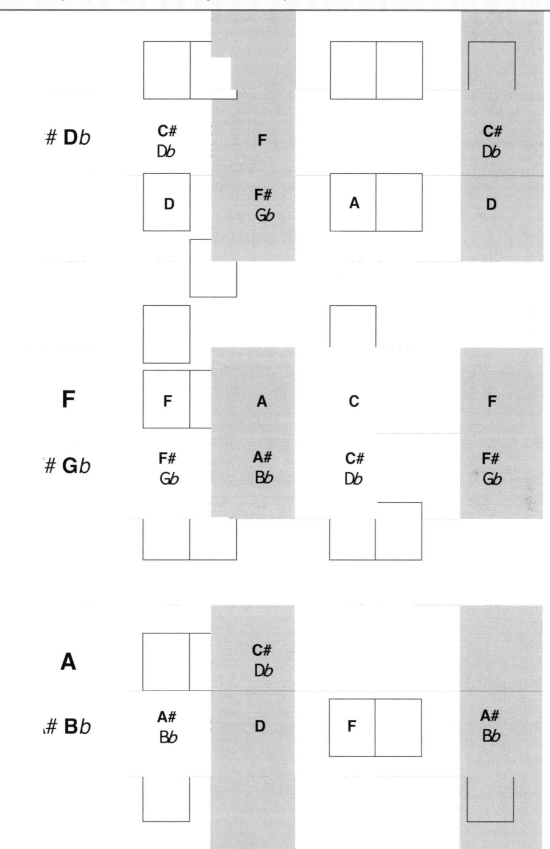

Axiom IV: To assemble the basic building blocks of a major chord in any specific key, you combine the *first*, the *third*, and the *fifth* notes of that scale in that designated key. This is called a Major Triad.

Notice I am singling out "major" chords in Axiom IV, and those chords are derived from "major" scales. Indeed, major scales are the only scales that we are considering in this Manual. Scales come in different configurations. Simply research "musical scales" on the Internet and you will discover a stockpile of information that will keep you busy for quite some time. But the goal is not to "keep you busy for quite some time." The goal of this Manual is to teach you how to play and understand the fundamental musical mechanics of what you are doing as you continue to master your instrument.

The Mechanics of Building New and Necessary Chords

Here are the "formulas" you will need to create major, minor, and other chords that apply to all the various progressions. I am using the Key of C in the following examples, but the mechanics relate to all keys. As a handy reference, I am presenting the C scale below:

C	D	E	F	G	A	B	C
1	2	3	4	5	6	7	8

NOTE: The symbol *b* represents a "flatted note." *b*3 = a flatted third, *b*7 = a flatted seventh, etc.

Major Chord - C
1, 3, 5 = C, E, G
This is the major triad.

Minor Chord - Cm
1, *b*3, 5 = C, E*b*, G
Here, we flat the third note of the scale which means we take that note down a half-step or a "semitone."

Seventh Chord - C7
1, 3, 5, + *b*7 = C, E, G + B*b*
Interestingly, even though it is called a "seventh," this chord does not feature the 7th note of the scale. The seventh chord is the combination of the major triad and the *flatted 7th note* of the scale.

Sixth Chord - C6
1, 3, 5, + 6 = C, E, G + A
The sixth chord is a new chord for us. I will chart out a C6 in the following pages and explain some of its uses. The sixth chord is the combination of the major triad and the 6th note of the scale.

Suspended Fourth Chord - C sus4
1, 3, 5 + 4 = C, E, G + F
The sus4 chord tacks on the 4th note of the scale to the triad. We have addressed the sus4 earlier, but we will look at other applications of sus4 *and* sus2 chords later in the *Manual*.

Suspended Second Chord - C sus2
1, 3, 5 + 2 = C, E, G + D
The same procedure as the sus4 except substitute the second note of the scale. Again, more on suspended chords later.

Major Seventh Chord: CM7
$1, 3, 5, + 7 = C, E, G + B$

The major seventh adds the actual 7th note of the scale to the triad to create this mellow-sounding chord that we have yet to consider. Several technical observations: The major seventh chord is designated as **CM7** with a capital **M** to signify that it is a *major* 7th. The minor seventh chord uses a lower-case **m** to signify that it is a *minor* seventh. Also, notice that the major seventh uses the true 7th note of the scale rather than the *flatted* 7th that is used in the seventh chord. I have always perceived major seventh chords as delicate, jazz-like chords. They are reasonably common in a variety of chart-topping songs. I am charting out a CM7 as well as an FM7 at the upper right to illustrate my point regarding the gentle, jazzy sound of these chords.

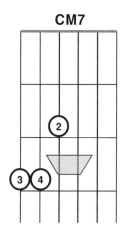 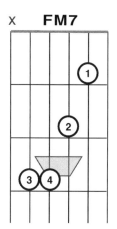

To get a feel for the M7 chords try rolling back and forth a few times with the CM7 & FM7. To some students this might sound familiar. Remember the band "America?" With these two chords you have most of their big hits just about figured out!

Minor Seventh Chord - Cm7
$1, b3, 5 + b7 = C, Eb, G + Bb$

Just like a standard minor chord, the third note of the scale is flatted to facilitate the minor, and just like a standard seventh chord, the seventh note of the scale is flatted and added to the *minor* triad. This yields the C minor seventh chord (Cm7). If the major-seventh chords evoke a mellow, jazzy feel, then the minor-seventh chords evoke a slightly darker, edgy feel. Unfortunately, it is extremely difficult to play a Cm7 on the first few frets— we will study the Cm7 in the Barre Chord section. Consequently, we will substitute an Am7 and a Dm7 to illustrate how these minor seventh chords sound.

Notes for Am7 = A, C, E + G
Notes for Dm7 = D, F, A + C

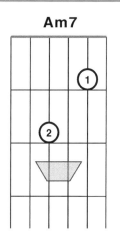 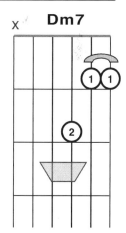

Alternate back and forth between these two chords for the "audio flavor" of the minor seventh. If you're feeling adventurous, toss in a G chord or an E chord and experiment with different sequences.

Revisiting the Sixth Chord - C6

1, 3, 5, + 6 = C, E, G + A

To illustrate the logic behind the structure of these 6th chords, I'm charting our old friend the C7 to the right along with the C6 chord. Notice that the note that defines the C7 a seventh chord is played by the fourth finger on the 3rd string at the 3rd fret. This is a Bb note which is the *flatted* seventh note of the C Scale:

C - D - E - F - G - A - **B** - C

To create the C6 chord from the C7 chord, you simply slide the Bb note down a half step to sound an A note which is the 6th note of the scale which creates the C6 chord.

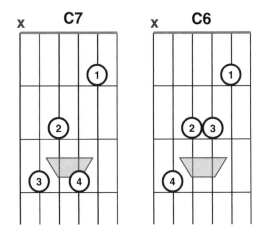

Creating a C6 from a C7 involves simple idea: Just slide down one note one fret. But this chord is difficult because it requires some tedious finger positions. There are alternative ways to play 6th chords that I demonstrate below.

Additional Examples of Sixth Chords

Below, I am charting four different sixth chords and a single A7 chord. The pale grey circles in four of the five chords shown represent the notes that defined the seventh chord. This note is dropped a half step to create the sixth chord. With the E chord, the defining seventh note (D) becomes a Db to facilitate the E6 chord and with the A7, the defining seventh note (G) becomes a Gb to facilitate the A6 chord. The Bb6 and the B6 are "up-the-neck" extensions of the A6 chord and can be carried up the fretboard to create additional 6th chords.

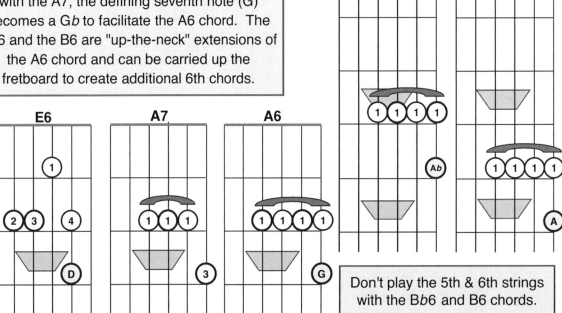

Don't play the 5th & 6th strings with the Bb6 and B6 chords.

Using Sixth Chords as a "Logical Example"

There are several points I want to highlight by focusing on the sixth chords.

First, I want to emphasize yet again that building chords is based on a logical matrix-based formula. The current example regarding sixth chords shows how to single out the flatted-seventh note that defines the seventh chord and drop it a half step to create the sixth chord. This is one of the many structural examples that is depicted in the information above.

Second, I wanted to comment on what I have called the "up-the-neck" extensions of the A6 chord. In the example above, we started with an A7 chord and rolled back the G note on the 1st string to create the sixth chord. We implemented this A6 by using the first finger as a "barre" to play the four relevant notes on the second fret. This handy little four-note structure makes it easy to slide the chord up and down the neck. That, in turn, illustrates how easy it can be to create new chords by moving a fixed structure up and down the fretboard. In the case of this A6 chord, what happens when we move it up a half step? It becomes an A#6 or a B♭6. Moving a chord up or down the neck is the same thing as moving an individual note up and down the neck. Accordingly, when you move the A#6 or B♭6 up another half step, you have a B6. You can readily see how you have learned some very complicated-sounding chords by a simple sleight of hand. This suggests some of the procedures essential to barre chords presented in the next chapter.

Third, by using these sixth chords as an example, I am able to expand on a theme we have considered throughout the *Manual*, notably, the sound and feel of different chords. Granted, trying to communicate how chords *sound* much less how chords *feel* is an extremely subjective task. It is particularly challenging, for example, to *write* about sound as "mechanical waves that are transmitted through a physical medium" and then go on to explain how these obscure waves impact our emotional sensibilities. Despite the shortcomings of *writing* about how we perceive certain sounds, there is a lesson to be learned with the sixth chords regarding the context of chords as they appear in songs and musical sequences.

In playing a sixth chord by itself, it seems to have a gentle sound—not the blue sound of a minor or the edgy sound of a seventh. It is simply a nice, relaxed texture. Played individually, the E6, A6, B6, and B♭6 are not particularly noteworthy chords and might even sound somewhat lost as if something was missing. If indeed something does sound "missing," it is not because the chord structure is lacking. What is missing is a sense of *context*. Put in the proper context, the E6, A6, B6, and B♭6 can make a dynamic musical statement. In other words, *the harmonic utility of a chord often depends on the company it keeps*. The following exercise illustrates the significance of *context* in the way certain chords *sound* and *feel*.

This exercise combines the four chords we have discussed above into a simple sequence that illustrates that context truly matters.

```
E6                  A6              E6                  B6      Bb6
/   /   /   /   /   /   /   /   /   /   /   /   /   /   /   /

A6                  B6     Bb6 B6  E6
/   /   /   /   /   /   /   /   /   /   /   /   /   /   /   /

E6                  A6              E6                  B6      Bb6
/   /   /   /   /   /   /   /   /   /   /   /   /   /   /   /

A6                  B6     Bb6 B6  E6
/   /   /   /   /   /   /   /   /   /   /   /   /   /   /   /
```

I hope that through this exercise, you can get a feel for the significance of chords in context. When coupled with some sympathetic and supporting "neighbors," many chords that sound somewhat bland when played solo come into their own as powerful support players in countless structures and progressions. Sometimes chords of this nature are called *passing* chords because they harmonically link the movement from one chord to another. We will explore other examples later in the text, but at this point, let us review the last axiom, **Axiom V**, that deals with the essence of progressions.

<u>Axiom V</u>: **To assemble the basic building blocks of a chord progression in a particular key, reference the three major triads based on the first, the fourth, and the fifth notes of that scale. This will yield the essential three-chord sequence of the harmonic series commonly called a chord progression.**

The gist of Axiom V comes down to the I-IV-V format we have referenced throughout the Manual. Communicating different chord structures through Roman Numerals or through Indo-Arabic Numerals (as in 1 - 10) is a handy and widespread method between contemporary musicians. It is certainly preferable to using traditional music terminology as depicted to the right. I find the notion of playing a "I-II-IV-V with a VI minor" much more accessible than playing a "Tonic-Supertonic-Subdominant-Dominant with a Submediant minor! Further, the number system is very helpful when applied to barre chords.

The following are *terms* that are common to standard musical notation in describing the "degrees" or positions of chords in a typical progression.	
I (One)	Tonic
II (Two)	Supertonic
III (Three)	Mediant
IV (Four)	Subdominant
V (Five)	Dominant
VI (Six)	Submediant
VII (Seven)	Subtonic

This concludes the Summation of Key Points Presented in the Matrix Method. The next page features a Transposition Chart that allows you to navigate different keys.

TRANSPOSITION CHART

This chart presents all twelve keys beginning with the Key of A. You can easily transpose notes or chords by locating the key you are in, then moving up or down the chart until you settle on your new key.

KEY

A	A#/Bb	B	C	C#/Db	D	D#/Eb	E	F	F#/Gb	G	G#/Ab
A#/Bb	B	C	C#/Db	D	D#/Eb	E	F	F#/Gb	G	G#/Ab	A
B	C	C#/Db	D	D#/Eb	E	F	F#/Gb	G	G#/Ab	A	A#/Bb
C	C#/Db	D	D#/Eb	E	F	F#/Gb	G	G#/Ab	A	A#/Bb	B
C#/Db	D	D#/Eb	E	F	F#/Gb	G	G#/Ab	A	A#/Bb	B	C
D	D#/Eb	E	F	F#/Gb	G	G#/Ab	A	A#/Bb	B	C	C#/Db
D#/Eb	E	F	F#/Gb	G	G#/Ab	A	A#/Bb	B	C	C#/Db	D
E	F	F#/Gb	G	G#/Ab	A	A#/Bb	B	C	C#/Db	D	D#/Eb
F	F#/Gb	G	G#/Ab	A	A#/Bb	B	C	C#/Db	D	D#/Eb	E
F#/Gb	G	G#/Ab	A	A#/Bb	B	C	C#/Db	D	D#/Eb	E	F
G	G#/Ab	A	A#/Bb	B	C	C#/Db	D	D#/Eb	E	F	F#/Gb
G#/Ab	A	A#/Bb	B	C	C#/Db	D	D#/Eb	E	F	F#/Gb	G

CHAPTER FOUR
Barre Chords

E Major Barre Chord Positions

Ascending E-Based Barre Chords

A Major Barre Chord Positions

Ascending A-Based Barre Chords

Your New Chord Inventory – Integrating the E and the A Barre Chords

Expanding Barre Chord Progressions

The C & the D as Barre Chords

The C Chord "Mini Barre"

The D as a Barre Chord

The C Barre with Other Cords

A Side Trip - Chord Voicings & Context

A Side Trip - Suspended Barre Chords

Ascending Asus4 & A Sus2 Chords

A Final Side Trip - The Sharp & Flat Progressions

The Twelve Major Key Scales

Conclusion

BARRE CHORDS

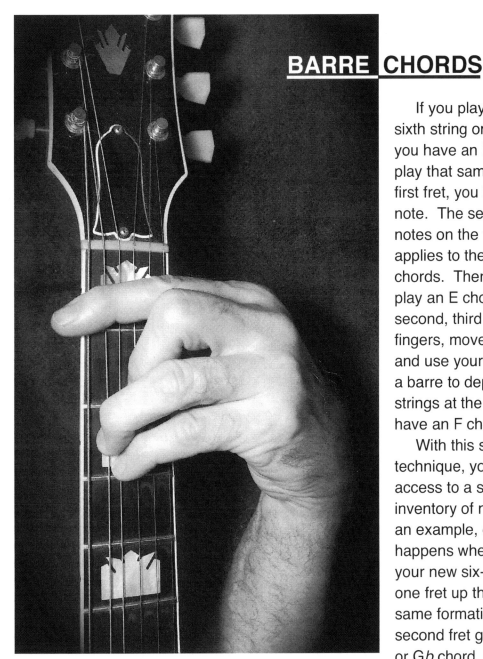

If you play the open sixth string on your guitar you have an E note. If you play that same string at the first fret, you have an F note. The sequence of notes on the fretboard also applies to the sequence of chords. Therefore, if you play an E chord with your second, third and fourth fingers, move it up one fret, and use your first finger as a barre to depress all six strings at the first fret, you have an F chord.

With this simple barre technique, you now have access to a substantial inventory of new chords! As an example, consider what happens when you move your new six-string F chord one fret up the neck. This same formation at the second fret gives you an F# or G♭ chord. If you proceed up the neck with the structure, the chords unfold in the same sequence as the notes on the E string. At the third fret you'll have a G chord, at the fourth fret you'll have a G# or A♭ chord and so on as you ascend the neck. As you can readily see, you've already learned a healthy collection of new sharp and flat chords, but this is just the beginning of the discovery process.

In addition to moving an E-chord structure up the neck to create new chords, you can also move an Em, an Em7 (which is essentially a minor chord with an added seventh note), or an E7 up the neck to create a new selection of chords. We will explore these possibilities shortly, but let's first consider some of the essential skills you'll need to master the barre chord technique. What follows are some key considerations and tips on how to play barre chords effectively.

105

• When I described playing the F chord in the barre-chord format on the previous page, I mentioned that you needed to play the E chord formation with your second, third and fourth fingers, move that configuration up one fret, and barre the remaining strings with your first finger. Obviously, if you're using your first finger as a "barre," you will have to use different fingers to facilitate the basic E chord. Using alternative fingering positions to create the basic chord structures that you will need to move the chords up the neck, specifically, the second, third, and fourth fingers, applies to most of the barre-chord structures that we will deal with in this chapter. Just to be clear however, I'm not

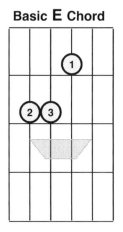
Basic E Chord

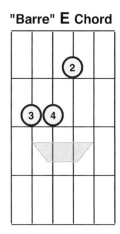
"Barre" E Chord

suggesting that you change the way you configure your basic chords like E, Em, E7 or A, Am, A7 and so on . . . Those fundamental first-position formations remain the same. As an example, I've charted out the fingering requirements for the basic E chord and the fingering requirement for barre chord in the illustrations above.

• A helpful way to envision the barre chord technique is to think of your first-finger "barre" finger as a "moveable nut." At the beginning of the *Manual*, I mentioned that the nut separates the fretboard from the headstock and the tuning machines. The nut serves several functions beyond just separating these two components of the instrument: It acts as a string guide to ensure that the strings are spaced properly as they travel up the fretboard; and it sets the strings at the

correct height above the fretboard. The illustration to the left highlights the nut at the end of the fretboard, and just to the left of the nut, there is an instrument called a capo placed at the second fret. A capo is a common guitar tool that allows you to raise the pitch of all the strings so that you can play your regular chords in a new position higher on the fretboard. If for example, you're playing a song in the Key of E and it's too low for the song you're singing, you can apply a capo and raise the pitch of all your strings to play the appropriate chords in a higher register. In this fashion, it is as if you're moving the nut from its original position, which of course you can't do, so you use a capo! Using your first finger as a barre accomplishes the same purpose which is why I mention the use of your first finger as a "moveable nut."

The basic rules we initially learned for forming regular chords apply to forming barre chords:

(1) Position your fretting fingers immediately behind the frets. If you place your fingers on the frets, it mutes the sound and if you place your fingers too far behind the frets, it creates a buzzing sound.

(2) Try to place your fingers perpendicular to the fretboard to avoid interfering with the adjoining fingers and strings.

(3) Apply adequate pressure to make each note sound clear and clean. It's much more difficult to apply these rules to barre chords when you're using your first finger as a barre. And, in many situations, you're working with a smaller fretboard space to form the proper fingering positions.

The illustration below shows the F barre chord. As you can see, the third finger doesn't quite snuggle up behind the third fret of the 5th string because the

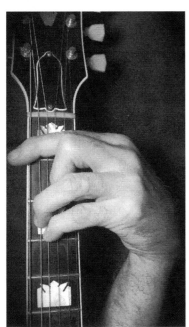

fourth finger is in the way. It's just close enough however to sound the note correctly. Also, the three fingers that form the chord don't appear to be completely perpendicular to the fretboard. The illustration to the right offers a better view of the fingers and their relationship to the fretboard. Although fingers two, three and four are not at 90-degree angles to the fretboard, these fingers have just enough of an angle to avoid conflicting with each other. Also, notice that the first finger (the barre finger) is slightly curved which is a product of applying the bulk of the pressure on the lower E (6th) string and the top B

(2nd) and E (1st) strings. This slight curvature is not a predetermined position I'm using to form the F chord, it's simply the configuration that works for me as I try to press down the appropriate strings on the first fret. I've found it helpful to subtly roll the first (barre) finger back toward the nut to incorporate the "boney" side of that finger to depress the strings. This is often preferable to using the soft, fleshy underside of the first finger. You can see the slight roll of the first finger in these photographs. Finally, in playing barre chords, you must apply considerable pressure on the strings to make sure they sound clear and clean. The best way to ensure maximum pressure is to pinch the neck between your thumb and your fretting fingers as illustrated to the right.

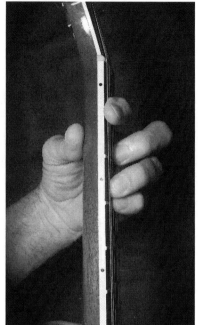

• In the final analysis, you're going to have to experiment with these various techniques to determine what works best for you. Again, there is no ultimate right way or wrong way to effectively execute these barre chords. Everyone's fingers are different, finger sizes vary, hand strengths vary, so as we move through the exercises that follow, be patient and try to establish a method that you find comfortable and efficient. The main goal is to create chords that allow each note to ring through crisp and clear.

• **Moving on to the Barre Chord Charts**: The first set of barre chords is based on the E major chord structure. After getting acquainted with moving the E chord up the neck, we'll address other variations of the E chord and integrate seventh chords, minor chords and minor seventh chords into the barre technique. We have yet to spend much time on minor seventh chords, so I'll make a brief introduction.

• **Introducing the Minor Seventh**: Minor sevenths are exactly what their label implies—a minor chord with a seventh rolled into the chordal structure. Like individual minor and seventh chords, minor sevenths have their own flavor and feel. From my audio perspective, adding a "seventh" (the flatted seventh note of the scale) to a minor chord adds a bit of a bite to the minor texture. Or, adding a "minor" (the flatted third note of the scale) to a seventh chord adds a blues-like texture to the sound of the seventh. Either way, minor sevenths are dandy little chords that add a new dimension to many progressions and chord sequences. The minor sevenths we will use in the forthcoming barre chord exercises are Em7 and Am7. There are certainly many other minor sevenths beyond the Em7 and the Am7, but we will focus on these two positions for now. By moving these chord templates up the neck with the barre-chord technique, we will create a healthy inventory of new minor seventh chords. I've charted the first-position Em7 and Am7 chords on the following page.

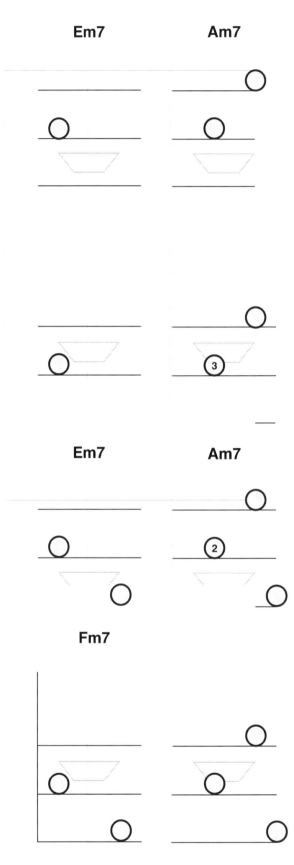

Em7   Am7

Em7   Am7

Fm7

These Em7 and Am7 fingering positions in the charts to the immediate left illustrate the original fingering positions for an Em7 and an Am7. To move these formations up one fret to play a barre chord, you must substitute different fingers to form the chord as illustrated in the subsequent six charts. In the case of moving the Em7 up one fret (which would yield an Fm7), you would use your third finger to play the designated note. In the case of moving the Am7 up one fret (which would yield an A#m7 or B♭m7), you would use your second and third fingers to play the designated notes. I've displayed these first-fret barre chords to the immediate left.

When we were learning seventh chords earlier in the *Manual*, we tried adding another seventh note in the higher register to give the chord an extra hint of "seventh spice." We can use that same technique with the minor seventh chords to produce what might be called an "accented minor seventh" chord. To the left are the Em7 and the Am7 in the first position with the added 7th in the upper register. With the Em7, we've added a D note—the flatted seventh note that makes the Em an Em7—at the third fret of the 2nd string. Similarly, with the Am7, we've added a G note—the flatted seventh note that makes the Am an Am7—at the third fret of the 1st string. These added notes accentuate the sound of the seventh. The final two chord charts to the left represent moving these formations up one fret with the first-finger barre to yield an Fm7 and an A#m7 or G♭m7 chord.

E Major Barre Chord Positions

The charts below provide the template that will be used in the barre-chord charts throughout the *Manual*. It is important therefore, to identify the key components of these charts. (1) The elongated matrix below represents the first twelve frets of the fretboard. The twelve notes situated at the left edge of the matrix represent a chromatic octave for the low E string. If you begin with an E note on the open 6th string and move up the fretboard one half step or semitone at a time, you'll arrive at the E octave at the 12th fret. (2) The bottom (6th) E

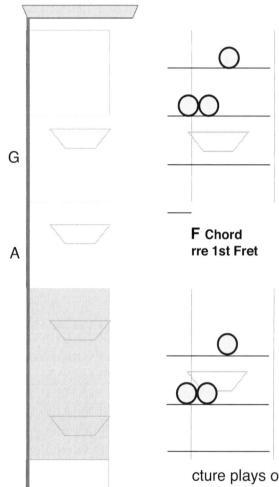

**F Chord
rre 1st Fret**

string in this matrix appears in bold relief because this chart focuses on the E-major barre-chord positions. As we've learned, the *notes* on the lower E string serve as our guide to the E-based *chords* as they ascend the neck. If you take an E *note* up a half step, you have an F *note*. If you take an E *chord* up a half step, you have an F *chord*. If you take that same F chord up another half step, you have an F# or Gb chord, and so on up the fretboard. (3) The numbers on the *right* side of the matrix (1-12) simply indicate the ascending frets. (4) The "'Basic E Chord" chart represents the fundamental chord that we will be using for this sequence of barre chords. (5) The "F Chord Barre" chart shows how the basic chord

cture plays out when it is moved up one fret and rred" to form a new chord. This same structure w ly as we move up the fretboard to form the F#-Gl rd, the G chord and so on up the neck. Please e that the fingers used to create the barre chord first finger as the barre plus fingers two, three, a) are different from those used to create the inal "first-position" chord.

This is our first adventure into the world of barre chords and to avoid any confusion about how the E-Cord Structure unfolds as it moves up the neck, I'm charting each individual chord in the E Major series from fret 1 through fret 12. This is a tedious illustration, but I want to make sure that there are no questions regarding the identity of each chord and its position on the fretboard. All of the chords below are formed with the first finger serving as the barre and the second, third, and fourth fingers forming the basic E-chord structure.

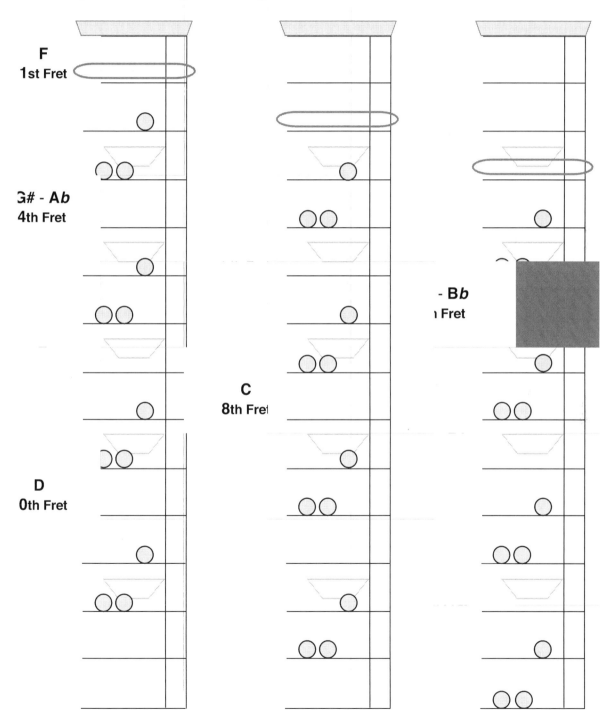

Congratulations! You've just learned an extensive assortment of new sharp and flat chords that would have been extremely difficult to play in the first position. These chords however, are simply the tip of the barre-chord iceberg. By learning these positions and how they systematically move up the neck, you now have access to a wide spectrum of new chord possibilities. Let me explain:

You now know how to play, for example, an F#-G*b* major by moving the E formation up to the second fret and using the first-finger barre. Knowing that, you can now play an F#-G*b* *seventh* chord, an F#-G*b* *minor* chord, an F#-G*b* *minor seventh* chord and a number of related chords rooted in the E major formation. I'll demonstrate with the following chord charts based on the F#-G*b* major chord:

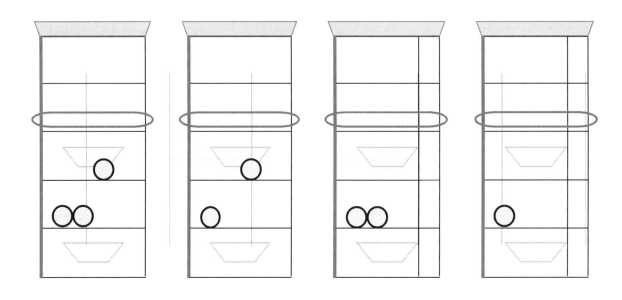

formation elevated to the second fret; the F#7-G*b*7 is the standard E7 taken up two half steps; the F#m-G*b*m is the standard Em at the second fret; and the F#m7-G*b*m7 is the Em7 at the second fret. To add a touch of the "seventh spice" we've mentioned, you can add another 7th note to the high register of the seventh and minor seventh chords as illustrated to the right. They're still F#7-G*b*7 and F#m7-G*b*m7 chords respectively; they simply have an enhanced seventh flavor.

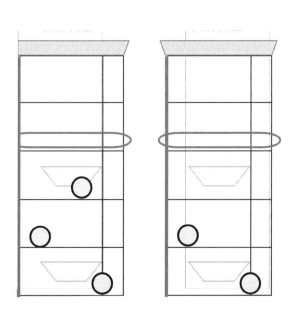

Ascending E-Based Barre Chords

These charts illustrate the chords created by advancing the fundamental chord formations for E7, Em, Em7, plus the "enhanced seventh" structures depicted at the top of each twelve-fret matrix.

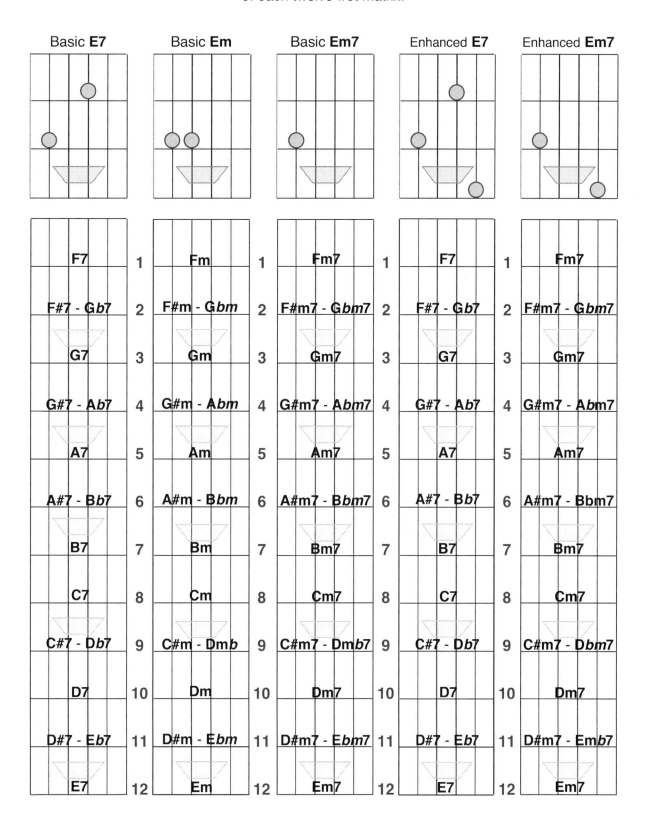

Once again, I must mention that several of the charts above are redundant. There are two F7 charts, one with the basic seventh structure and the other with the enhanced seventh structure, and the same holds true for the two Fm7 charts. I present these redundant charts to highlight the different "voicings" of these chords. I wanted to make sure that I illustrated how all of the chords and their respective voicings played out as they moved up the fretboard.

A Major Barre Chord Positions

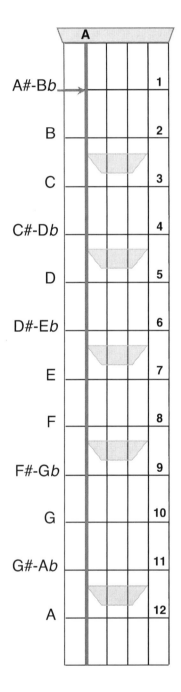

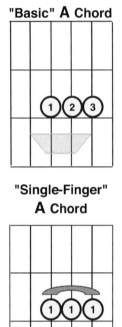

"Basic" A Chord

"Single-Finger" A Chord

The same fundamentals that govern the barre chords based on the E-chord structures also govern the barre chords based on the A-chord structures. We will now use the A string as our reference string. Notice that it appears in bold relief in the extended matrix. The individual notes that appear to the left of the matrix represent the ascending notes of the A (5th) string.

The fundamental chord structure we will use to create the forthcoming barre chords is the A chord. As you'll recall, there are two fingering options for the A chord: (1) The "basic" formation that requires three fingers (fingers one, two, and three) and (2) the "single-finger" formation that requires your first finger to sound the three appropriate notes. To facilitate the A Major barre chords, either version is acceptable . . . It ultimately depends on your personal comfort level. Keep in mind that to use the "basic" formation in the barre chord format, you will have to use fingers two, three and four because your first finger must be used as the barre. To use the "single-finger" formation, you'll have to use your third finger to sound the proper notes because once again, your first finger serves as the barre. Each approach has its pluses and minuses, so experiment with both techniques and consider the explanations and illustrations below.

Using the "basic" formation for the A barre chords can be challenging because you must pack three fingers (fingers two, three, and four) into a tight space while maintaining a solid barre function with your first finger. This configuration is depicted in the chart below on the left which depicts an A# or Bb chord. Using the "single-finger" formation for the A barre chords can be challenging because you must be careful not to interfere with the high E (1st) string with your third finger. This configuration is represented in the chart below on the right and depicts the same A# or a Bb chord. To avoid interfering with the high E (1st) string you must arch back your third finger at the first knuckle just enough to avoid touching the E (1st) string. I suggest trying to master both of these configurations because they each have structural advantages depending on the context in which they are used. We will now move on to some derivatives of the basic A-chord structure and take these new chords up the neck.

ıasic A-Barre ormation for **A# - B***b*	ɟle-Finger nation for \# - B***b*

ST-FINGER BARI   FIRST-FINGER BARRE

All of the A-structure barre chords aren't as structurally tedious as the initial "basic" or "single-finger" A major formation. What follows are other A-based structures. The initial set of charts (from left to right — A7; Am; Am7; Enhanced A7; Enhanced Am7) indicating the fingers that you'll use when you're playing barre chords beyond the first position. In other words, these five initial charts are not intended to be "first position" charts.

Enhanced A7   ∃nhanced **Am7**

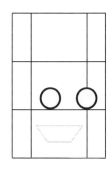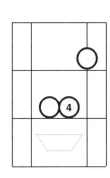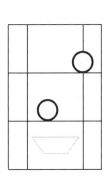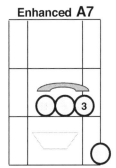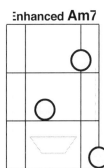

Before applying these A-based formations for seventh, minor and minor seventh chords to the barre chord system, we will revisit the original A-major structure and see how the "base" chord travels "north" on the fretboard. The charts below are similar to those that we used to illustrate how the E major chord played out when it was advanced up the neck from fret 1 through fret 12. Once again, I want to make sure that there are no questions regarding the identity of each A-based barre chord and its position on the fretboard. All of the chords below are formed with the first finger serving as the barre and the third finger forming the necessary A structure. Feel free to use the 2nd, 3rd, and 4th finger format in forming the A structure if that technique is more comfortable.

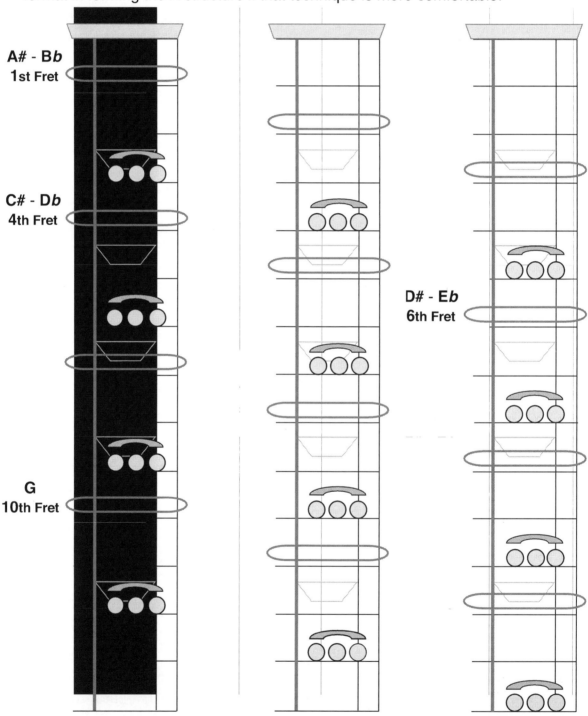

A# - B♭
1st Fret

C# - D♭
4th Fret

D# - E♭
6th Fret

G
10th Fret

Ascending A-Based Barre Chords

These charts illustrate the chords created by advancing the fundamental chord formations for A7, Am, Am7, plus the "enhanced seventh" structures. The template for each ascending chord is depicted at the top of the appropriate twelve-fret matrix.

Basic **A7**	Basic **Am**	Basic **Am7**	Enhanced **A7**	Enhanced **Am7**

Basic **A7**		Basic **Am**		Basic **Am7**		Enhanced **A7**		Enhanced **Am7**	
A#7 - Bb7	1	A#m - Bbm	1	A#m7 - Bbm7	1	A#7 - Bb7	1	A#m7 - Bbm7	1
B7	2	Bm	2	Bm7	2	B7	2	Bm7	2
C7	3	Cm	3	Cm7	3	C7	3	Cm7	3
C#7 - Db7	4	C#m - Dbm	4	C#m7 - Dbm7	4	C#7 - Db7	4	C#7 - Db7	4
D7	5	Dm	5	Dm7	5	D7	5	Dm7	5
D#7 - Eb7	6	D#m - Ebm	6	D#m7 - Ebm7	6	D#7 - Eb7	6	D#7 - Eb7	6
E7	7	Em	7	Em7	7	E7	7	Em7	7
F7	8	Fm	8	Fm7	8	F7	8	Fm7	8
F#7 - Gb7	9	F#m - Gmb	9	F#m7 - Gmb7	9	F#7 - Gb7	9	F#m7 - Gbm7	9
G7	10	Gm	10	Gm7	10	G7	10	Gm7	10
G#7 - Ab7	11	G#m - Abm	11	G#m7 - Abm7	11	G#7 - Ab7	11	G#m7 - Amb7	11
A7	12	Am	12	Am7	12	A7	12	Am7	12

Your New Chord Inventory
Integrating the E and the A Barre Chords

When you think about all the new barre chords you've learned with all of their respective seventh, minor, and minor-seventh adaptations, and then roll in all of the new sharp and flat positions into the mix, you've created a considerable new bag of tricks! Consider for a moment the following points:

- You can now play all the major chords . . .
- You can now play all the minor chords . . .
- You can now play all the seventh or minor-seventh chords . . .
- You can now play all the major, minor, seventh or minor-seventh chords in any sharp or flat configuration . . .[13]

This is a significant leap forward! If a particular song requires a Gbm7, a C#7, an Ebm, or an F#, no problem! With only a brief reference to your new barre-chord charts, you're there!

Granted, it will take a little time to internalize these various positions, but the nature of the fretboard matrix is very logical and the fundamental sequence of ascending or descending notes doesn't change. With the E and A barre-chord structures you've learned thus far, you should focus on the note sequence of the E (6th) string and the A (5th) string. Essentially, it's as simple as "A-B-C," or in this case, A through G with the appropriate sharps and flats sprinkled in the right spots to flesh out the seminal "DNA Tonal Twelve-Pack!"

This brings us to a new and exciting realization about the relationship between the E-based barre chords and the A-based barre chords and how to blend these structures into easily accessible progressions and chord sequences. This "E-A" relationship highlights the logic and simple beauty of the matrix method and will help you build progressions, learn the songs you want to learn, create your own material, and expand your skills in playing along in impromptu performance settings. To illustrate this relationship, we'll begin an exercise based on a simple E chord in the first position.

There are two goals in this exercise. **The First Goal** is to play a basic 1-4-5 progression in the Key of E. That's simple enough. Start with your E chord, give it a few strums, move to the A chord for a few more strums. You can use the original three-finger method or the single-finger method. Complete the progression with a B chord formed by using the A-barre chord technique.

---

[13] I'd like to qualify the claim about being able to play "all the [various] chords." I'm not trying to say that you can now play each and every major, minor, and minor-seventh chord that there is. As we've learned, there are many different ways to play the same chord . . . there are different "voicings" and positions of the same chord for example. What I am saying is that you can now play a practical and accessible version of every major, minor and minor-seventh chord.

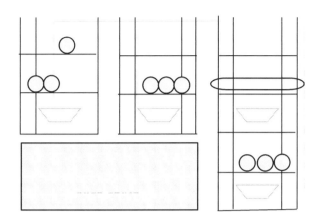

In this case that involves using the one-finger A chord technique moved up to the fourth fret with your first finger as the barre on the second fret. This three-chord I-IV-V progression is illustrated to the left. Try playing the progression in sequence with four strums on the E, four ͏͏͏͏͏͏͏ ͏͏͏ A f ͏͏͏

on the A and then begin the sequence again. Your main challenge ͏ making the transition from the A to the B an͏ matter of practice so keep at it until your chͼͼͼ ͼͼͼͼ͟ͼ͟ͼ͟ ͼͼͼ ͼͼͼͼͼ ͼͼͼ ͼͼ͟ entire progression moves at a steady pace.

   The Second Goal of this exercise is to play a simple I-IV-V progression in the key of Bb. That's right, Bb, but don't panic! With the barre chord technique, it's stunningly simple. By combining the E-based and the A-based barre chords, you can play this intimidating progression in a compact formation in the middle section of the fretboard. The essential idea is to move the E-based chord structure up the neck to create the Bb chord which serves as the starting point for the progression.

   With your first finger providing the barre immediately behind the sixth fret, place your second finger on the 3rd string at the seventh fret, place your third finger on the 5th string at the eighth fret, and your fourth finger on the 4th string at the eighth fret. This barre position yields the Bb chord which is the tonic or the "I" chord of the Bb progression. You can now move to the subdominant chord or "IV" chord of the progression with a basic finger position shift. Keep your first-finger barre at the sixth fret and convert your E-based barre structure to an A-based barre structure by using your third finger to depress the 2nd, 3rd and 4th strings at the eighth fret. This yields the appropriate Eb chord that satisfies the requirement for your "IV" chord. To create the dominant or "V" chord, simply slide the "IV" structure up two frets. Make sure you maintain the exact same IV-chord structure as you move your barre from the sixth to the eighth fret. This yields the F chord which is the proper "V" chord for the Bb progression. In this fashion, you can play an entire "I-IV-V" sequence in what amounts to a handy little box-like structure that involves moving your barre finger only two frets! I've charted these three chords on the following page.

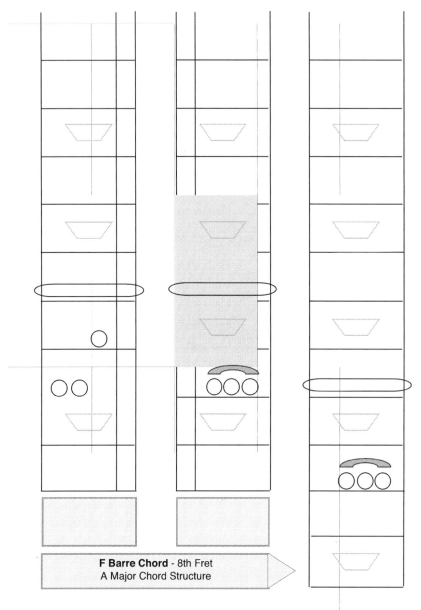

F Barre Chord - 8th Fret
A Major Chord Structure

building a progression in Bb is a relatively easy ta using the barre chord technique. Once you've established your root chord with the E-major formation, switch to the major formation to produ the IV chord then slide t structure up two frets to produce the V chord to complete the progressio

The same technique holds true for building progressions based on the various notes situate on the E (6th) string. If you want to play a three chord F progression, yo apply the technique at th first fret. If you're workir on a three-chord song in with your band and it's t high for the singer, appl the technique at the second fret to drop the tune to the key of F#-Gb

The chord progressions based on the E-major barre structure that are supplemented with the A-based barre structures move up the neck in the same way that the individual notes on the E (6th) string move up the neck. If you can play a G#-Ab note at the fourth fret on the bottom E string, then you can play a G#-Ab progression at that same position. You now have the ability to play fundamental **I-IV-V** progressions in any key. All the notes on your lower E string easily translate into a new chord progression.

With this in mind, I'd like to make a suggestion that's been helpful to students over the years: Make a "note ribbon" for your lower E string. A note ribbon (which is my term, so it's not official music "lingo") is a thin piece of masking tape that runs the length of the guitar neck from the headstock to the body of the instrument which identifies the individual notes on the lower E string. Cut a strip of standard masking tape that will stretch from head of your guitar to the body, about 14" to 19" long. It needs to be long enough to cover the first twelve frets of your guitar and should be between ¼ and ½ inches in width. I suggest masking tape rather than other high-tech tapes because it's easy to write on masking tape with a felt-tip pen *and* it won't damage the finish on the neck of your guitar when you take it off. Once you've situated the long strip along the top side of the neck along the fretboard where it's readily visible, label the strip to correspond to the individual notes on the E string. Again, *use a felt tip pen*; not only because it's easy to write with on masking tape but because a ballpoint can make an impression in the finish of your guitar. The ribbon provides you with an instant reference to all of the progressions you can create based on the E major barre formation. Here's an image of my homemade note ribbon.

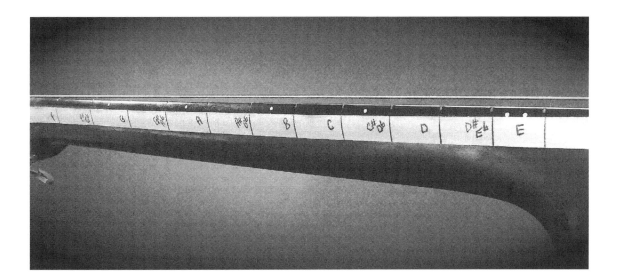

Expanding Barre Chord Progressions: In the previous section, I discussed building progression in advanced positions on the fretboard in a compact space. I described this technique as "a handy little box-like structure that involves moving your barre finger only two frets!" This is a good way to envision a fundamental I-IV-V progression based on the barre chord method. You might call it a "**Barre-Box Progression**" or a "**Barre-Box Structure!**" When I consider the quirky way I learned how to play the guitar—picking up tips here and there by listening to records, watching bands, jamming with my friends, and occasionally checking out an instruction manual—I realize that I've always visualized the relationships between strings, notes, and chords in geometric terms. I saw the D chord as a small triangle, the D7 as an inverted triangle, the A chord as a small block, and the G7 chord as a forty-five-degree angle from the low E string to the high E string . . . These are just a few of the geometric parallels that came to my mind as a young student. These visions of chords and note sequences as shapes came into sharper focus with the barre chord structures. That's when the matrix concept began to take shape. I came to realize that by sliding this formation up, moving that structure over, or dropping some other configuration down a few frets, I could do all kinds of productive things. These geometric revelations are helpful in expanding the "Barre-Box Progression" concept. To illustrate how sliding, moving, or dropping this, that, or the other can increase you options in creating progressions, we'll begin by adding the relative minor to our barre-box structure.

As a rule of thumb, to create the relative minor for a I-IV-V barre-box structure based on the E-major chord structure, simply drop the "I" chord three frets and change it to a minor chord. To illustrate this technique let's begin with a C barre chord on the eighth fret. Move the C barre chord down three frets and you have an A barre chord. Remove your second finger from the chord structure and you have an Am chord which is the relative (VI) minor for the key of C. Round out your I-VIm-IV-V sequence by sliding your barre back up to the eighth fret and forming the A-based structure to create the F (IV) chord. To complete the progression, slide that complete structure up to frets to the tenth fret to create the G (V) Chord.

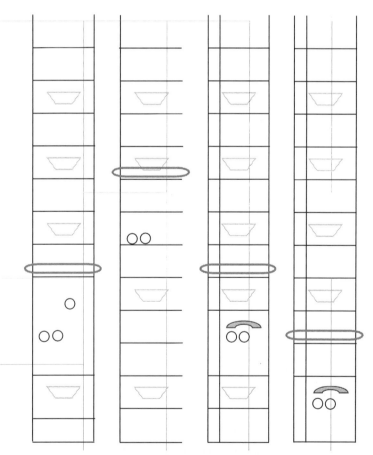

As these charts illustrate, you have an accessible four-chord progression in the middle regions of the fretboard. One of the most helpful aspects of this box-barre arrangement is the ease with which you can create new progressions in other keys. If, for example, you wanted to create a I-VIm-IV-V progression in the key of C#-D*b*, you would simply slide this entire formation *up* one fret. Similarly, to create a I-VIm-IV-V progression in the key of B, you would simply slide this progression *down* one fret.

There are two minor setbacks to the barre-box I-VIm-IV-V structure: First, in the upper reaches of the fretboard there is not enough room to squeeze in the chords. The C-major position at the eighth fret offers adequate room for all four chords as does the C#-D*b* position at the ninth fret even though it might be a bit cramped for some players. Beginning with the D position at the tenth fret though, the space between frets becomes a determining factor. A great deal of your ability to create barre chords in the upper register depends on the size of your hands and your comfort level with operating in "close fretboard quarters." Nonetheless, the theory behind the barre-box structures applies up the neck until you run out of frets. This brings us to the second minor setback regarding these barre-chord structures.

On the lower reaches of the fretboard, rather than running out of room, you run out of frets. On and below the third fret, there's not enough "fret room" behind the barre to facilitate the three-fret drop for your relative minor chord. You can certainly play the three-chord I-IV-V progressions like the F progression at the first fret, the F#-G*b* progression at the second fret, and the G progression at the third fret. But you can't make the three-fret drop to create the relative minors for the F and F#-G*b* progressions. You can create the relative minor, Em, for the G progression, but when you drop back three frets from your G barre position, you no longer need your first-finger barre because the guitar nut takes its place. Technically therefore, it's not a barre chord.

Despite these minor setbacks, the Box-Bar Structure is tremendously helpful and opens up a range of new chords and progressions. And, as we continue to move through the barre chords, you'll find that there are other configurations for the chords you'll need up and down the neck. Let's consider, for example, the Am structure and how it might apply to the relative minor barre chords for the keys of F at the first fret and F#-G*b* at the second fret. Rather than use a barre chord that's based on the E structure, we'll use a barre chord that's based on the Am structure.

The chart to the right presents two major scales, one for the Key of F and the other for the Key of F#-G*b*. The relative (VI) minor for F is Dm and the relative (VI) minor for F#-G*b*

F	G	A	A# B*b*	C	D	E	F
F# G*b*	G# A*b*	A# B*b*	B	C# D*b*	D# E*b*	F	F# G*b*

is D#m or Ebm. On the extended matrix charts below, I've illustrated the tonic (I) chords and their relative (VI) minor chords in each particular key *on the same chart* to economize space. The first chart represents the F chord at the first fret and its relative minor, Dm, at the fifth fret. The second chart represents the F#-Gb chord at the second fret and its relative minor, D#-Eb minor at the sixth fret. In these cases of creating the relative minor by using the "Am" barre formation, you need to move **4 frets up** from your base (I Chord) position and use the Am barre structure. This stands in contrast to creating the relative minor chord by using the Em barre structure which requires a move **3 frets down** from your base (I Chord) position. These examples highlight the utility of the barre-chord methodology. It is a technique that offers alternative and accessible ways to create the chord you need for the mission at hand.

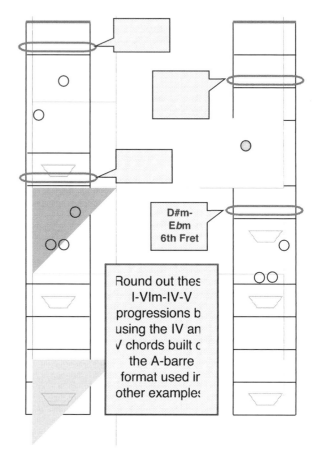

D#m-Ebm
6th Fret

Round out these I-VIm-IV-V progressions b using the IV an √ chords built c the A-barre format used in other examples

Keep in mind that we've been working with two basic structures in crating our barre chords: The E chord formation and the A chord formation along with their various derivatives—minor chords, seventh chords and minor seventh chords. Generally speaking, the tremendous variety of chords you can create with these two fundamental barre-chord structures—the E structure and the A structure—will satisfy most of your practical needs in playing all varieties of songs, progressions, and formations. To illustrate this point, let's consider our collection of basic first-position chords from the A chord through the G chord, and see how they relate to the principles of barre chords.

• The A Chord: We've already covered the mechanics of moving the A chord and its derivatives (Am, A7, Am7) up the fretboard.

• The B Chord: The B chord in the first position on the lower fretboard is nothing more than the A chord moved two frets or two half steps up the neck. The first-position B chord is already a barre chord.

• The C Chord: The C chord is one of the first-position chords that can be used effectively in advanced positions on the fretboard. We will explore some of these possibilities in the next section.

• The D Chord: The D chord is another one of the first-position chords that can be used effectively in advanced positions on the fretboard. We will also explore possibilities for the D chord in the next section.

• The E Chord: We've already covered the mechanics of moving the E chord and its derivatives (Em, E7, Em7) up the fretboard.

• The F Chord: Like the B Chord, the F Chord in the first position is nothing more than an E Chord moved one fret or one half step up the neck. The first-position F Chord is already a barre chord.

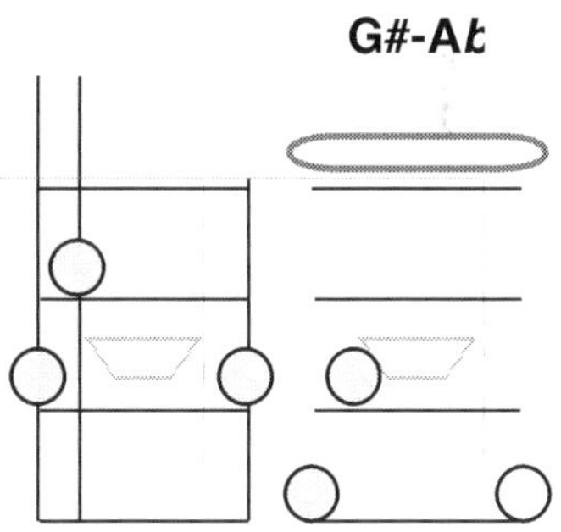

• The G Chord: Theoretically, you can take the standard first-position G Chord up the fretboard to create new barre chords, but it requires some very tedious fingering gymnastics. To take the G structure (depicted to the right) up the neck, your barre must be positioned two frets behind the required fingering positions. Check out the chart to the far right that illustrates taking the G chord up one fret. Notice that you must first play the required notes with your second, third and fourth fingers because you'll need your first finger for the barre, and, to further complicate the effort, that barre must be two frets behind the fingering structure. It's a tough configuration to play effectively. Fortunately, it's really not worth worrying about because of the extensive inventory of barre chords that are already available through the techniques we have studied thus far. There are plenty of options available to create the chords you need without worrying about taking the first-position G chord "north."

G#-Ab

The C and the D as Barre Chords

C#-D*b*
X Barre 1st Fret

C#-D*b*
Mini-Barre

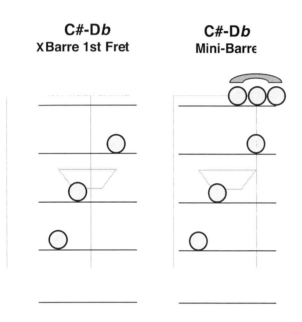

C Chord Heads "North:" Many of ... players I've worked with over the ...s often take the C chord up the neck ...eate a new set of functional chords. ...can be done in two ways. You can ... the C chord just like the E or the A ...d, move it up the fretboard and apply ...irst-finger barre behind the main ... of the chord. Or you can move the ...e basic C chord up the neck by using ...t might be called a "mini-barre." This ...lves using your first finger to barre ...1st, 2nd, and 3rd strings and not ...er with applying the barre to all six ...gs. This is the technique that seems ...r players. Either technique will ...certainly get the job done and I've displayed both options to the upper left.

Are there advantages of one technique over the other? In my opinion, the full-barre technique is more difficult to play, but it does give you access to all six strings. I will address the utility of playing all six strings in a side trip later in this section. The mini-barre technique is easier to play and still allows you the option of using your fourth finger to create an alternating bass line between the 5th and 6th strings. (We discussed alternating bass lines in the "Pick & Strum" section on page 45.) Choosing one barre technique over another depends on your comfort level with either the full barre or the mini-barre. Personally, I prefer the mini-barre. With that in mind, let's see what happens when we take the C chord north up the neck.

• **The C Chord as Barre Chord**: Like the E chord and the A chord, the C chord is a good candidate for a barre chord. It doesn't have the versatility of the E or the A—the standard C structure doesn't lend itself to an easy transformation from a major and to a minor for example—but this popular chord does display certain unique characteristics in advanced positions on the fretboard. To ensure that you have a clear picture of how the C formation unfolds as it travels up the neck, I'm introducing the following charts. I begin with the C chord in the first position and highlight the subsequent chords as it moves north using the "mini-barre." The "reference string" for the C barre-chord sequence is the A string which appears in a bold type. Finally, please note that the low E (6th) string is not played in this barre-chord sequence.

The C Chord "Mini-Barre" Sequence from the Chord's "First Position" at the Nut Through the Eleventh Fret

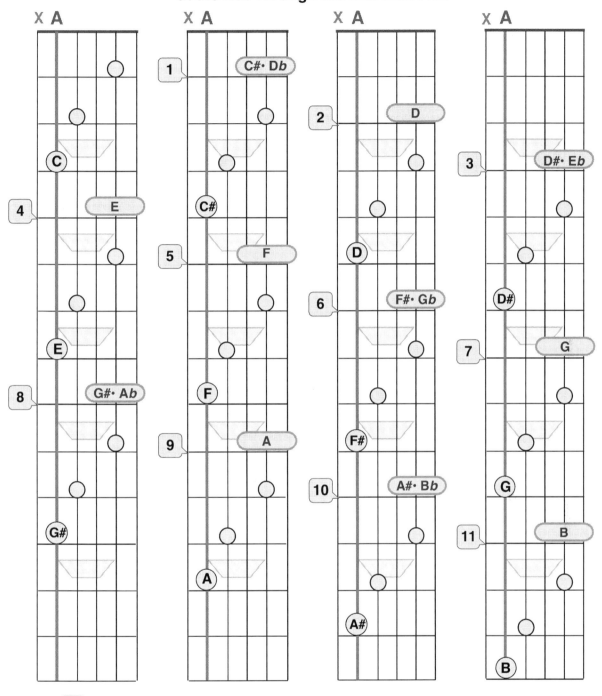

1 ⌐ Represents the fret position

◯ Represents finger placement

Ⓒ Represents finger placement and the root note of the barre chord

(C#· D♭) Represents the position of the mini-barre & the chord designation

• **The D as a Barre Chord**: Using the D chord as the foundation for a full six-string barre chord is not a practical consideration. There are several reasons for this. **First**, to take the D-chord "triangle" up the neck by using the standard six-string barre requires some difficult finger placements. The chart to the right illustrates the mechanics of taking the basic D chord up one fret and apply-ing the full six-string barre on the first fret to create the D# or E*b* chord. This fingering challenge rivals the "difficulty factor" of moving the full G chord up the neck to create a G# or an A*b* (see p. 124). Taking the D "triangle" up the neck with a the six-string barre is simply not a user-friendly chord structure. **Second**, there doesn't seem to be any pressing need to use this difficult formation in light of all the other barre chords available, particularly the E & A formats. **Third**, the basic concept of moving the D "triangle" up the fretboard has already been done by taking the C chord up the fretboard. Let me explain: If you take a C chord, move it up two frets (a whole step) and use the mini-barre, you have the D chord that's depicted in Chart 1. In that D chord, finger three plays an F# and finger four plays a D (see Chart 2). If you drop finger three (the F# note) and finger four (the D note), you are left with the configuration in Chart 3 with the mini-barre, the second finger playing a D note and an open A and D string. If you release the mini-barre and simply play the 1st and the 3rd strings along with the D note on the third fret of the 2nd string, you will recognize the familiar face of our old friend, the basic D chord depicted in Chart 4.

FINGER BARRE

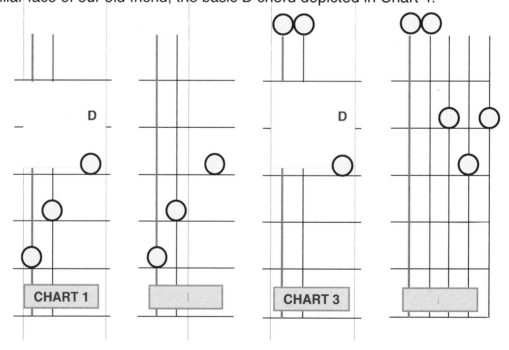

CHART 1

D

CHART 3

D

There are two points I'd like to make regarding these charts. First, I wanted to illustrate another example of the logical nature of the guitar. When you "dust off some of the fluff" from the C chord that was taken up two frets to create the D in the **CHART I**, you end up with the basic D chord that we learned in the early pages of the *Manual*. The "fluff" I'm referring to in this case includes the "third-" and "fourth-finger" notes in the C-based mini-barre chord at the second fret. Generally, these are essential notes in the C-based barre formation. They are essential in playing a C# or D*b* on the *first* fret and they're essential in playing a D# or E*b* on the *third* fret, and they are essential to most of the advanced positions on the neck. But given the way that the fretboard matrix is laid out, they are optional when the C formation is taken to the second fret. When you remove your fourth finger from the 5th string, you have an A note and when you remove your third finger from the 4th string, you have a D note and both of these notes are compatible with the basic D-chord triad—D, F# & A. This brings me to the second point. The standard D chord that's depicted in **CHART 3** and **CHART 4** above (either fingering technique will work) is nothing more than a C barre chord on the second fret with the "fluff removed!" Consequently, the structure we've been referring to as the "C barre chord" structure can be used quite nicely as a "D barre chord" structure, provided of course, you include the "fluff" in your fingering positions up and down the neck. Knowing this, there is no need to wrangle with the extremely difficult fingering requirements necessary to take the D chord "triangle" up the fretboard with the full six-string barre.

• **The C Barre with Other Chords – A Working Example**: The charts on the next page present three C-based barre chords—an E chord, an F# chord, and an A chord—that are combined with other E-based and A-based barre chords and several first-position chords. This yields a new melodic rhythm pattern, a pattern that we have not previously considered. With the term, "melodic rhythm pattern," I'm suggesting (1) that the sequence is a collection of rhythm guitar chords, (2) that those chords, when played in the prescribed order, produce a subtle melodic theme, and (3) that the sequence has a characteristic rhythmic feel. The "rhythmic feel" I'm referring to is created by an easy-going strumming technique which I call a "*strum and* pattern." This pattern simply means that you make a two-stroke strumming move by gently striking the designated strings of a chord with a downward motion, then lightly rake over the same strings as you bring your hand back up to begin another strum.

To begin this exercise, we will chart all the chords we will be using. Although we have studied many of these chords before, either as barre chords or as first-position chords, I'm mapping out each chord and its position because this particular progression unfolds at all points of the fretboard. Because several of the chords are situated in the higher registers, I'm using an abbreviated chord chart that *begins on the fret immediately before the first-finger barre.* This is best explained by presenting our first three chords and addressing each structure individually.

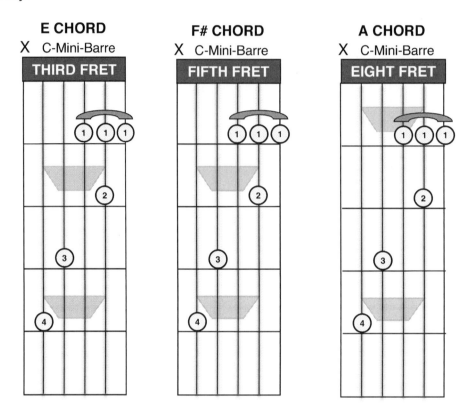

The E chord formed with the C-barre formation actually begins on the fourth fret with the three-finger mini-barre. The notation in the dark box at the top of the chart, "THIRD FRET," is simply an indicator of your relative position on the fretboard. Your second finger falls on the fifth fret of the 2nd string to sound an E note which is a root note of the chord. Your third and fourth fingers fill out the basic C-structure. The F# (or Gb) chord is the same structure advanced two frets up the neck. The mini-barre falls on the sixth fret. Once again, your second finger sounds a root note (F#-Gb) at the seventh fret of the 2nd string. With the third chord, the mini-barre for the A chord falls on the ninth fret. And again, your second finger sounds a root note (A) for the chord. I mention the "second-finger" notes in these chords because I often use these notes on the 2nd string as a reference point for C- and D-based barre chords and for various lead guitar patterns I play from time to time. Also, your fourth finger on the 5th string sounds the same root note one octave below the second-finger note on the 2nd string. This is another valuable reference so please study the sequence of notes on the 5th (A) string and the 2nd (B) string just as you have learned that sequence on the high and low E strings. Here are six more barre chords for the exercise:

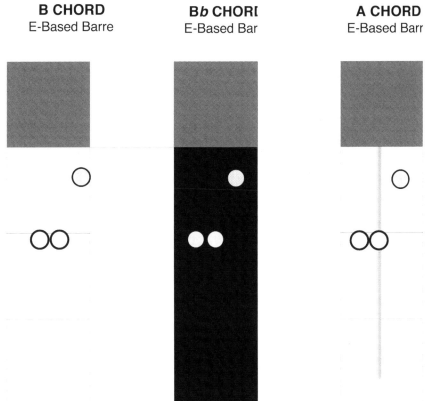

B CHORD
E-Based Barre

Bb CHORD
E-Based Bar

A CHORD
E-Based Barr

Please note that in the charts on this page, we are revisiting our E-Based and A-Based Barre Chords. Also, the placement of the Fret Markers in all twelve of these chord charts are accurate and provide another reference to the proper position on the neck.

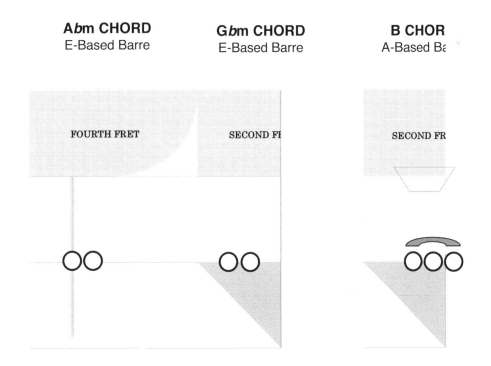

Abm CHORD
E-Based Barre

Gbm CHORD
E-Based Barre

B CHOR
A-Based Ba

FOURTH FRET

SECOND FR

SECOND FR

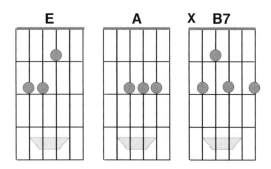

These last three chords are routine first-position chords. They round out the twelve chords we will be using in the following exercise. One of the basic ideas behind this effort is to incorporate C-based mini-barre chords, E- and A-based barre chords and simple first-position chords. The following exercise ("Sixteen Bars in E Major") incorporates all three chord formats.

This exercise is a sixteen-bar progression. Each bar has four beats, each line has two bars so there are eight beats per line. Each beat represents one downward strum of your instrument. Remember that we will be using a "*strum-and*" technique. This requires that after you play the downward stroke, you lightly sound the strings on the upstroke of each strum. The ampersand (the "**&**" symbol) represents the upstroke or the "and" movement. The twelve chords we'll be using, as they are charted above, are represented by the following symbols:

The E chord formed with the C-mini-barre	**E**(Cmb)
The F# chord formed with the C-mini-barre	**F#**(Cmb)
The A chord formed with the C-mini-barre	**A**(Cmb)
The B chord formed with the E standard-barre	**B**(EB)
The B*b* chord formed with the E standard-barre	**B*b***(EB)
The A chord formed with the E standard-barre	**A**(EB)
The A*b*m chord formed with the E standard-barre	**A*b*m**(EmB)
The G*b*m chord formed with the E standard-barre	**G*b*m**(EmB)
The B chord formed with the A standard-barre	**B**(AB)
The first-position E chord	**E**
The first-position A chord	**A**
The first-position B7 chord	**B7**

I realize this might appear to be a cumbersome collection of chord symbols to consider but try to take it one chord at a time as you work through the progression laid out on the next page. Don't worry about trying to memorize the individual symbols. Try to visualize the structure of each chord as it appears on the fretboard . . . Try to internalize the half step and the whole steps between the various structures, and you'll discover a logical and manageable series of chords. The exercise is in 4/4 time and it moves along at a relaxed pace. There are a number of new chords, there are challenging chord changes, and there are positions up and down the neck, so take it slow and easy.

Sixteen Bars in E Major

E(Cm*b*)   **F#**(Cm*b*)

/ & / & / & / & / & / & / & / &

A(Cm*b*)   **B**(EB)   **B***b*(EB)

/ & / & / & / & / & / & / & / &

A(EB)   **A***b*m(EmB)   **G***b*m(EmB)   **B**(AB)

/ & / & / & / & / & / & / & / &

E   **A**   **E**   **B7**

/ & / & / & / & / & / & / & / &

There are several new elements to this progression. First, instead of a straight-ahead I-IV-V format, this series of chords is a I-II-IV-V format. The II chord is a pleasant addition to the progression and reflects the chord structures of many popular songs. The initial chords of "Eight Days a Week" by The Beatles comes to mind. Second, the one-step descending increments between the B (V) chord and the A (IV) chord—specifically, B to B*b* to A—is a nice touch. This "fret-by-fret" chord-changing capability is another helpful feature of the barre chords. Third, the descending minor chords (A*b*m to G*b*m) that follow the A (IV) chord is an innovative way to set up the B (V) chord in the third line. This two-chord sequence illustrates that full chords as well as single notes can be used to segue from one section of a progression to another section. The arrow at the end of the progression indicates that after the final B (V) chord, you should circle back to the top and begin again. Keep moving through the progression until you can maintain a relaxed, steady pace. Once you have a workable grasp of this sequence, try to incorporate some of the innovations in this piece to other songs and sequences you might be working on.

• **A Side Trip - Chord Voicings & Context**: The practice of taking a standard C chord up the neck with the full first-finger barre offers me an opportunity to expand on some important points we've addressed earlier in the text. With the full-barre technique, you can play all six strings of the C chord. But, as you know, we've always treated the C as a five-string chord. The bottom E string is usually not played in the C and it's reasonable to assume that the lowest string would not be used in taking the chord up the neck. From a technical aspect however, the lower E note is a legitimate part of the C chord. After all, the highest note in the chord is an E note—the open E on the 1st string. Plus, the E

133

is an essential note in the basic C-chord triad—C, E & G. So why is the lower E bypassed in our standard first-position C chord? That question might best be answered by playing the chord.

When I strum a C chord that includes the lower E note on the open 6th string, I get the feeling that something might be out of place. This particular configuration, when played alone with no support chords, sounds somewhat dark. I sense a tension in the lower register of the chord. The reason for this perceived *dissonance* has to do with the concept of *voicing*.[14] We explored this term in our discussion about the idea of "first-position" chords on page 63. For your convenience, I'm reprinting that passage below.

> The idea of a "first-position" chord suggests another important term. That term is "**voicing**." To play a chord in the first position is to play a chord in a certain "voicing." To play that same chord in another position further up the neck is to play it another "voicing." When you play the standard C chord in the first position, you play the following five notes in the following order: C, E, G, C, and E. A variation of the same chord played higher on the neck might begin with a G note followed by C, G, C, E, and C. Still another variation even higher on the neck might begin with an E note followed by G, C, E, and C. Each of these variations or "voicings" present their individual notes in a different order. Additionally, each voicing sounds at a different pitch relative to its position on the fretboard. Although they're all C chords, each chord voicing produces a singular texture, sound, and feel.

Stated differently, the perception or "flavor" of a chord is not only created by the specific notes that you play or where you might position that chord on the fretboard; that perception can depend on the order of the specific notes in the chord. This explanation applies to our C with the low E note as the first note in the chord. By striking the E note first, you've compromised the "comfort zone" of the average listener because most listeners (or players) are conditioned to hear the C note first. Beginning the chord with that big and booming E note is an audio curveball! Still, this slightly strange C chord does have a place when played in the proper **context**. I'll present two chord passages to illustrate these observations.

---

[14] It might be helpful to comment on the term "dissonance." To describe a chord or a musical passage as "dissonant" is to imply that it sounds unstable or that the tension between its aural components requires some sort of resolution . . . Something sounds "off" and needs to be fixed! Dissonance depends largely on the listener and their cultural conditioning. Different musics from around the globe are built on different scales and timing signatures that in turn suggest a variety of perceived "good" or "bad" sounds. What might sound dissonant or grating to an accomplished guitarist in New York City, might sound like the harmonies of Heaven to the sitar player in New Delhi, India.

First, we'll try a basic group of chords—C, F & G—that illustrate the dissonant nature of the "E-based" C chord:

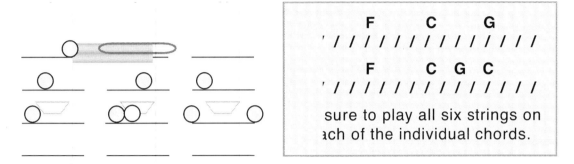

F   C   G
' / / / / / / / / / / / / /

F   C G C
' / / / / / / / / / / / / /

sure to play all six strings on
ach of the individual chords.

This basic I-IV-V progression should illustrate what I'm calling the "perceived dissonance" in the basic C chord when played with the chords that it's most commonly associated with. As you can hear in working through this series, the F and the G chords hold up fine, but coming from and returning to the hybrid C chord creates a degree of "tonal tension."

We'll now move to a new configuration of chords that demonstrates how the "E-based" C chord can blend in nicely with other chords and enhance the feel of a specific harmonic sequence. I've assembled several chords into a little riff rooted in E minor. There is no special song I'm referencing in this sequence. The riff is just a group of chords that I felt blended well to illustrate the utility of the hybrid C chord we're discussing. I hope that you'll sense a stronger compatibility between our "E-based" C and the supplemental chords. We'll be working with our hybrid C and fou

Em	C	Am	G	D
sic chord	w/ Low E	basic chorc	basic cl	asic chord

Play these chords in the order they appear above and use the rhythm pattern defined below. This exercise has three parts and in this initial segment, use simple downward strums playing all six strings with the exception of the final D chord which requires the omission of the lower E (6th) string. Also, notice that the final two chords in the sequence, G and D, receive only one strum each to complete the two eight-beat lines charted below.

```
Em          C[+E]        Am          G      D
/      /     /     /      /     /     /      /
Em          C[+E]        Am          G      D
/      /     /     /      /     /     /      /
```

In this segment of the exercise notice that the low E note remains a constant in the first three chords— Em + C + Am. Please notice that I'm including the symbols "+E" in brackets to remind you to play the open E note in the C chord. This is *not* a standard musical notation, simply a friendly reminder. Beginning each of these three chords with the same E note lends continuity to the sequence and the move to the G chord for a single strum (with a G note in the bass) and the D chord for a single strum (with the A note [the open 5th string] in the bass) rounds out this driving, minor-flavored pattern with two upbeat major chords wrapping up each eight-beat line. Because the open lower E note plays a prominent role in this series, we're going to adjust our standard D chord to include a playable note on the lower string in the next phase of the exercise. We will also modify our strumming technique to create a different rhythmic interpretation of this five-chord combination.

The low 6th string plays an important role in four of the five chords above. It remains open during the first three chords, moves up to a G note with the G chord but is silent in the standard D chord. As the second part of this exercise, we're going to add an F# note on the 6th string of the D chord to facilitate its use in the chord sequence. Plus, that F# note will be played in an unconventional

way. You're going to play the F# note with your thumb. Yes, that's right, *with your thumb*. Such a move may not be accepted practice when playing the classical guitar, but as a "fly-by-the-seat-of-your-pants" rock 'n' roll dinosaur, I'm a great believer in thumbs as well as many other unconventional techniques. It's quite simple: Play the regular D chord "triangle" with fingers one, two and three, then reach around the neck with your thumb to play the 6th string on the second fret to sound the appropriate F# note. As you'll readily realize, you can't play this note with the "tip" of your thumb . . . You need to use the fleshy part of your thumb, but in this case, it gets the job done. I'm offering an image of this somewhat strange chord configuration (above right) as well as a chord chart for this D chord with an F# in the low register (below).

Despite its uncommon structure, this is a big, warm-sounding chord that will serve you well in your future performance and writing adventures. For our current purposes, the added F# bass note enables you to play all six strings of the D chord which in turn allows you to play all five chords of this sequence in their six-string formats. We will now modify our strum pattern to take advantage of this full six-string capacity.

D
w/ F# Bas

Rather than playing these five chords with a simple downward strum, we'll initiate a strum *down* then a strum *up* movement. In the previous exercise, after completing the "strum-down" motion we immediately returned our strumming hand to the "ready" position to make the next downward stroke. In this segment, we'll use what might be called a "*strum-and*" technique. Instead of returning the strumming hand to the ready position after the downward stroke, we'll rake the pick across all six strings on the way back up to the starting position. This upward strum falls on the "and" part of the natural "one *and* two *and* three *and* four" count. To play this *strum-and* technique, you don't need to make a heavy-handed effort to play the strings on the upswing of your strum. You simply need to acknowledge

A Side Note: This D chord with the F# in the bass is essentially just a D chord I've seen this chord identified in differer ways depending on its voicing or on the theoretical standards of the person naming the chord. By exploring variou: chord charts in books or on the Internel you might find chords you recognize with different names. That's fine, but you should be more concerned about how you use your new chords and blen them into the sounds you want to make and learn the songs you want to play. Still, I strongly recommend that you research all sources—instructional books, the Internet, other players or teachers—for new chord voicings or fingering positions. The technical name of a particular chord is secondary to using that chord. **Follow your ears** to discover the music you want to learn.

those strings with a light brush of the strings. This *strum-and* stroke is as much about timing and feel as it is about highlighting the six individual notes you're playing during your upward strum. Try playing these five chords with this strumming technique. Notice that I've added the "F#" reminder to the D chord in the chart below. Playing this sequence with the *strum-and* method will require the upstrokes that are designated by the "&" symbol which I've presented in a lighter gray text. Also notice that the last two chords, the G and the D [+F#] are single strokes.

Em		C [+E]		Am		G	D [+F#]
/ &	/ &	/ &	/ &	/ &	/ &	/	/

Em		C [+E]		Am		G	D [+F#]
/ &	/ &	/ &	/ &	/ &	/ &	/	/

In playing this chord sequence, you might sense that the designated upstroke seems to make it move with a crisper feel. The cadence for the *strum-and* stroke doesn't need to be faster than the single stroke method—Playing this riff at approximately 100 beats per minute will do nicely for both strumming configurations. (Remember, you can easily reference an online metronome by simply searching "metronome." I highly recommend practicing with a metronome. It will definitely *improve your groove*!) Playing the last two chords, G and D, with single down strokes is designed to accent the final chords of the line and create a sense of finality before beginning the sequence again. This single-stroke finish is a matter of taste, so if you'd rather "double-stroke" these chords, then please press on!

For the third and final phase of this exercise, I'll introduce a new strumming method that involves a quick downward stroke which focuses on the lower register while muting the strings with the base or the fleshy part of your picking hand. There are three phrases in this sentence that deserve clarification:

1. "A quick downward stroke:" This refers to what I call a "single-chop" strum. It's a quick downward motion that covers a select few strings rather than all six strings. In the *strum-and* stroke exercise above, you strum all six strings on the down stroke and rake the same strings on the up stroke. With the "single-chop" strum you play two quick down strokes for each *strum-and* motion. Stated differently, the "*strum-and*" exercise above for the opening Em chord requires a count of "one, *and*, two, *and*" which translates into a "down, *up*, down, *up*" movement. The "single-chop" stoke for the Em requires a count of "one, two, three, four" which translates into four rapid down strokes.

2. "The lower register:" These single-stroke strums focus on lower strings of a particular chord. There are several reasons for this focus, the first being the easy availability of the lower strings. Because you're only trying to play two, three or possibly four strings, it makes sense to start with the E(6), A(5), & D(4) strings that are the most accessible. Another reason rests with the idea of beat or percussion. The single-chop style is a blend of rhythmic and tonal effects. This is best illustrated in the opening formats of a couple of popular tunes: "Just What I Needed" (1978) by The Cars and "Every Breath You Take" (1983) by The Police. The opening verses of both tunes illustrate the single-chop feel by setting up the rhythm and groove and by setting up the basic chord changes. In "Just What I Needed," the electric guitar presents an excellent example of the chop-stroke rhythm. In "Every Breath You Take," Sting's bass line lays down the series of percussive eighth notes while the guitar presents a chop stroke rhythm accented by a series of arpeggiated chords that reinforce the groove. Both of these songs are worth listening to in the "single-chop" context.

3. "Muting the strings:" This is a new technique that once again seems to contradict one of our earlier rules regarding allowing the notes we play to ring

through crisp and clear. Nonetheless, it's a tried-and-true technique that helps us accentuate the blend of percussion and tonality that we're trying to create with the single-chop method.

In the image below I've illustrated the position of the right hand and how the fleshy part of the hand gently rests against the saddle of the bridge. For a more pronounced muting effect, roll your hand towards the sound hole and for less pronounced muting effect, roll your hand back to create less contact with the strings.

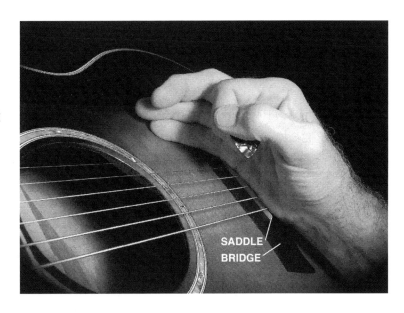

So why bother muting the strings? The primary reason is to create another tool for your bag of tricks to reproduce certain sounds and textures that are common in the world of popular music and to better equip you for original material you might want to create. This technique is helpful in laying down solid rock 'n' roll and R&B rhythm tracks as in the songs mentioned above. It's a familiar component in country recordings, heavy metal hits, and an extremely popular practice in live-performance settings. After you're acquainted with the technique, you'll probably notice it more and more in your personal music selections and your adventures in listening to live music.

Begin by trying the single-chop strum with a single Em chord. This will enable you to get the feel of the technique . . . Do you like more or less of the mute effect? Are you comfortable with playing three or four strings in your single down stroke? Sometimes, playing only two strings might yield a sound that appeals to you. You might like to vary the degree of muting by gently rolling the base of your hand on and off the saddle. These are all aspects of the technique you can experiment with by using a single chord to get the feel of the chop strum. When you're comfortable with the Em, apply the method to other chords in the exercise. Notice the "and" (&) symbol has been replaced by a single chop stroke (a right slash) and the last two chords, G and D, ring out as single chords:

Em	C[+E]	Am	G	D[+F#]
/ / / /	/ / / /	/ / / /	/ /	/ /

Em	C[+E]	Am	G	D[+F#]
/ / / /	/ / / /	/ / / /	/ /	/ /

> Don't play the light gray "ghost strokes" at the end of each line. Simply *count* them.

When I play this sequence with the single-chop method, it seems to take on a more aggressive vibe than the same sequence played with the down and up stroke. I've used this technique on countless occasions in the studio and on stage particularly when I'm trying to establish a hard-edged rockin' groove. The technique reminds me of a ruff & tumble old steam engine chugging down the tracks. The muting technique is also helpful as a volume control for electric guitar players. I've found that I can crank up my guitar and with the muting technique, I can produce an explosive sound that I can control with the degree of muting I choose to use. By releasing the mute, I can play an accent chord or a riff that cuts through for a brief interval that doesn't "hog" too much "audio space" because I can immediately "re-mute" the guitar to settle back into the steady groove. The technique enables you to play staccato chord or notes. Staccato refers to rapid, brief, or "clipped" sounding chords or notes. As an example, try playing the four chords is a lively sequence: E, D, A & G. Strum the E chord with a strong, quick stroke and immediately mute it. Repeat this quick "strum & mute" for all the chords while keeping a steady beat. This quick series of chords played in this fashion produces an unusual and striking contrast to simply strumming from one chord to the next. All in all, the variety of muting techniques make for some very dynamic audio options and sound textures. Such options are also very compatible with the acoustic guitar. I encourage you to experiment and "keep an ear out" for these techniques as you listen to the music you like.

As I mentioned above, I had no specific song in mind in sewing these five chords together. The two tunes I mentioned previously, "Just What I Needed" and "Every Breath You Take" illustrate the chop-strum method but don't necessarily reflect the chords in our exercise sequence. If this configuration reminds you of a special tune, you might look it up on the Internet and try to adapt what you've learned in this lesson to the structure of the song you've found.

• **A Side Trip - Suspended Barre Chords**: In the pages above, I mentioned that the many of the suspended fourth and suspended second chords are extremely difficult to play in the first position and are much more accessible by using barre chord techniques. (See pp. 57-61, "Suspended Chords.") The following charts lay out those techniques. The fundamental structure for these suspended chords is the A-based barre chord. As you will see, it's necessary to use fingers two, three and four to form the chords rather than using the single third finger that is often used in the A-based barre structure.

Ascending Asus4 & Asus2 Chords

These charts illustrate the chords created by advancing an Asus4 and an Asus2 up the fretboard. The template each ascending suspending chord is depicted at the top of the appropriate twelve-fret matrix.

Asus4 **Asus2**

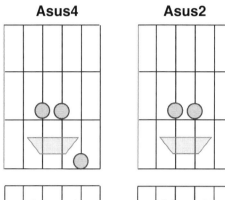

The basic structures for the Asus2 and the Asus4 are charted to the right and below. The two templates below actually represent a Bsus4 and a Bsus2 because the barre is situated on the second fret. Please note that fingers two, three, and four are used to form sus4 chords and fingers two and three are used to form sus2 chords.

Bsus4 **Bsus2**

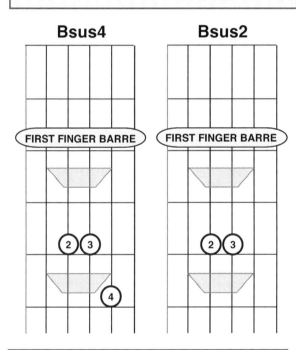

FIRST FINGER BARRE   FIRST FINGER BARRE

The lines to the right of the Matrix Charts on the right represent the fret numbers. Fret One on the Asus4 chart represents the placement of the fist-finger barre to yield the A#sus4 or Gbsus4. Even though the A major chords are not picture here, remember that you can easily move from a sus4, to the major, to the sus2 and so forth by repositioning your fourth finger.

Asus4 matrix	#		Asus2 matrix	#
A#sus4 / Bbsus4	1		A#sus2 / Bbsus2	1
Bsus4	2		Bsus2	2
Csus4	3		Csus2	3
C#sus4 / Dbsus4	4		C#sus2 / Dbsus2	4
Dsus4	5		Dsus2	5
D#sus4 / Ebsus4	6		D#sus2 / Ebsus2	6
Esus4	7		Esus2	7
Fsus4	8		Fsus2	8
F#sus4 / Gbsus4	9		F#sus2 / Gbsus2	9
Gsus4	10		Gsus2	10
G#sus4 / Absus4	11		G#sus2 / Absus2	11
Asus4	12		Asus2	12

• **Summing Up the Barre Chords**: Technically speaking, you can take any first-position chord up the neck and craft a barre chord. Simply move a specific structure "north" on the fretboard, place your first finger the proper distance behind it and you're ready to go! Although it is theoretically "simple" to "move a specific structure 'north' on the fretboard," it is often extremely difficult to "place your first finger the proper distance behind" that chord. We demonstrated that challenge in trying to advance the first-position G chord up the fretboard. It proved to be tough (and largely unnecessary) business.

I've seen classically trained guitarist who have astounding "barre-technique" skills. Their approach to the use of their fretting hand coupled with their exceptional dexterity enables them to place a barre at any accessible position on the neck and play a variety of chords, notes, runs or complicated sequences with their available three fingers. It's as if they set their first-finger barre and have the mental and physical wherewithal to essentially forget about it while the remaining fingers operate as independent agents. This skill is the reification of a point that I made earlier regarding the use of the first finger as a "moveable nut," a technique that could be called an "organic capo." Classically trained guitarists at this advanced level make it look like their fretting hand operates on two independent circuits whereby once the barre is set, the second circuit kicks in to enable the remaining three fingers to cut loose and create engaging chords and note patterns. Personally, my left hand operates on a single circuit, but I still try to experiment with setting a barre and forming innovative structures. I strongly encourage you to try some similar experiments and exercises.

The most practical application of the barre-chord technique lies in using the E-chord structure, the A-chord structure, and to a lesser degree, the C-chord structure. The E and the A formations offer the greatest versatility because they are easily modified to create minor, seventh, minor seventh, major seventh, and sixth chords at positions up and down the fretboard. The C-based and D-based structures also have their unique utility. One of the great advantages in mastering barre chord techniques is the expanded access to many, many new chords, chords that are often all but inaccessible in the first position.

• **A Final Side Trip – The Sharp and Flat Progressions**:

On page 17, when I was introducing "Chords and Chord Progressions," I mentioned that our focus would be on progressions associated with the "whole tones." Then I went on to say, "The whole tones and their subsequent progressions are A, B, C, D, E, F, and G," and that we would consider the progressions rooted in "sharp" and "flat" keys later in the *Manual*. At this time, I would like to address the "sharp" and "flat" progressions. The progressions for the keys of A#-B*b*, C#-D*b*, D#-E*b*, F#-G*b*, and G#-A*b* follow the same structural guidelines as the progressions for the Keys of A, B, C, D, E, F, and G. We will use the Key of A#-B*b* as an example. Here is the A#-B*b* scale:

The first note of the scale, (A#-B*b*) is the I chord or the Tonic, the fourth note of the note of the scale (D#-E*b*) is the IV chord or the Subdominant, the fifth note of the scale (F) is the V chord or the Dominant, and the sixth note of the scale (G) is the relative minor. The logical parallel between the sharp & flat progressions and the whole tone progressions is very straight forward, so you might wonder why I have waited to single out this information in a belated Side Trip. I did so for the following reasons:

• To illustrate that the fundamental structural rules (Axioms) regarding chords and progressions apply across the board to all notes regardless of the symbols (# or *b*) they might carry.

• When we began studying the fundamentals of chords and progressions we were dealing exclusively with first-position chords, and . . .

• Many of the chords that would have been necessary to round out the progressions in sharp and flat keys would have been practically impossible to execute in the first position, so . . .

• I had no convenient way to illustrate or chart many of the chords that would have been necessary to play many of the sharp and flat progressions without the use of barre chords, and with that in mind . . .

• I decided it would be better to wait until you understood the structural mechanics of progressions and chords depicted through the five Axioms presented in the Matrix Method Chapter . . .

• And, most importantly, that you could use the barre-chord methodology in creating the chords for these progressions.

With these tools at your disposal, charting out all the sharp and flat chord progressions should be well within reach. For your convenience, I've reproduced the chart, "The Twelve Major Key Scales" below.

THE TWELVE MAJOR KEY SCALES

Notice the shaded positions: These are shaded to remind the reader that in forming major scales there is always a half-step between interval 3 & 4 and 7 & 8.

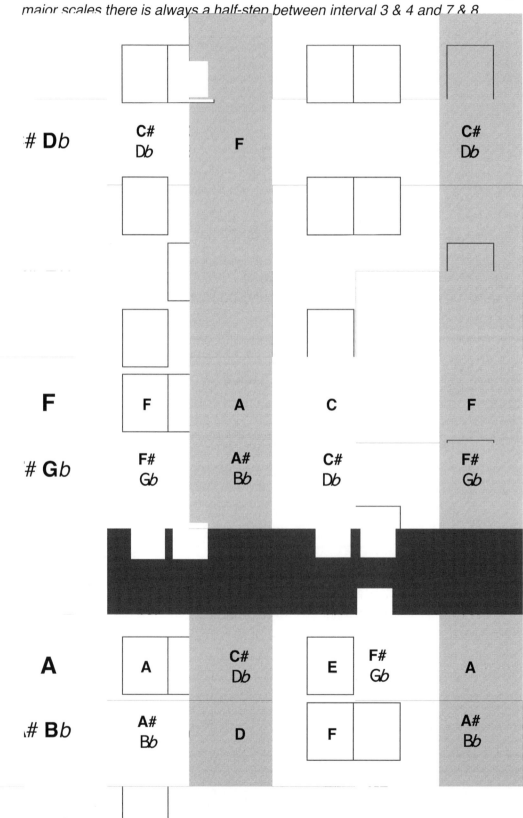

CONCLUSION

This concludes the *initial version* of the *Matrix Manual*. I say the *initial version* because there is still a great deal of material to be covered and I've considered writing additional chapters for the book. In fact, I've tentatively begun work on several new topics:

I. "Tablature, Tabs, 'Tab-Talk' & Techniques" explores the world of guitar tabs, which is a contemporary form of "charting" or writing out popular songs. Guitar tabs are extremely popular on the Internet. The inquisitive, tech-savvy guitar player can find Internet guitar tabs for everything from "The Star-Spangled Banner" to the latest from Lady Gaga or from Stephen Foster's "Camptown Races" to the new country hit by Kenny Chesney!

II. "Notes, Noodling & Lead Guitar" focuses on the use of single notes, scales, runs and lead guitar riffs and playing techniques. "Noodling" or "Noodling Around" is an informal term used by many guitar players to describe improvising guitar lines in real time which essentially boils down to pulling hot licks from your shredder's inventory and piecing them together on the fly to create unique lead guitar segments.

III. "Tricks of the Trade" is a potpourri topic featuring advanced lead licks, innovative playing techniques, unique chord combinations, the use of effect pedals and other practical performance and recording techniques.

IV. There is also a section on "Musical Radar" which deals with anticipating chord changes in unfamiliar songs and the art of "playing by ear." This is essentially a discussion about striving and thriving on stage and in the studio by using the techniques I've covered in the *Matrix Manual*.

Before I dove in and invested the time and effort it would take to write and illustrate several new chapters, I thought I'd see how this version went over in the marketplace. I really wanted to gauge the reactions of those who were brave enough to slog through this extended tutorial. If the response was good, then I'll press on with the additional topics. With that in mind, I'd like to know what you think. I'd like to know what you liked or didn't like. I'd like to know how you think

I could improve the *Matrix Manual*. You can email me at: hilliscd@gmail.com. I'd love to hear from you.

I'm confident that the material we have covered thus far provides you with the fundamental tools you will need to recreate the popular songs you want to play, write the tunes you want to write, and make the music you want to make. The sections on music and audio theory, as long-winded and cumbersome as they might have seemed, enables you to "speak music" and "talk audio" with your bandmates and musical contemporaries. A shared jargon—a common language based on commonly shared concepts—is essential to making quality music with others.

I encourage you to explore the Internet for alternative interpretations of the material we've covered, for answers to questions you might have, or for new avenues of study. Cyberspace is an excellent source for examples and tutorials in easily accessible formats. Given the seemingly limitless material available online, it's truly a great time to be learning the guitar.

I encourage you to develop dialogues with your fellow players, participate in any and all jam sessions, try to play with more advanced musicians as well as those who are less advanced. It's all good . . . It's all productive. But most importantly, play, then play some more. That's the best path forward.

Thanks so much for reading the *Matrix Manual for Guitar*, and I wish you the very best in your forthcoming adventures. I sincerely hope the *Manual* has been helpful.

Cheers,

Craig D. Hillis

Austin, Texas
November 2021